ALTERNATIVE FUTURES FOR WORSHIP
Baptism and Confirmation

ALTERNATIVE FUTURES FOR WORSHIP

Volume 2

Baptism and Confirmation

Volume Editor

MARK SEARLE

Authors

MARK SEARLE
ANDREW D. THOMPSON
HERBERT ANDERSON
GAIL RAMSHAW-SCHMIDT
ROBERT D. DUGGAN
STEPHEN HAPPEL

THE LITURGICAL PRESS
Collegeville, Minnesota 56321

Cover design by Mary Jo Pauly

Manufactured in the United States of America.

ISBN 0-8146-1494-9

1   2   3   4   5   6   7   8

Library of Congress Cataloging-in-Publication Data

Alternative futures for worship.

    Includes bibliographies.
    Contents: v. 1. General Introduction / volume editor,
Regis A. Duffy ; authors, Michael A. Cowan, Paul J.
Philibert, Edward J. Kilmartin — v. 2. Baptism and
confirmation / edited by Mark Searle ; by Andrew D.
Thompson . . . [et al.] — v. 3. The eucharist / edited
by Bernard J. Lee ; by Thomas Richstatter . . . [et al.]
— [etc.]
    1. Sacraments (Liturgy) 2. Catholic Church—Liturgy.
I. Lee, Bernard J., 1932–
BX2200.A49   1987   265   86-27300
ISBN 0-8146-1491-4 (set)

CONTENTS

THE CONTRIBUTORS

MARK SEARLE is associate professor of theology at the University of Notre Dame and a past president of the North American Academy of Liturgy.

ANDREW D. THOMPSON, formerly associate professor of personality and religious development at The Catholic University of America, is currently consulting and writing in Washington, D.C.

HERBERT ANDERSON is professor of pastoral care at Catholic Theological Union in Chicago and a pastor of The Evangelical Lutheran Church in America.

GAIL RAMSHAW-SCHMIDT is a scholar of liturgical language and president of The Liturgical Conference.

ROBERT DUGGAN, pastor of St. Rose of Lima Parish in Gaithersburg, Md., has written and lectured widely on the Rite of Christian Initiation of Adults.

STEPHEN HAPPEL, associate professor of religion and culture in the department of religion and religious education at The Catholic University of America, has recently published (with James J. Walter) *Conversion and Discipleship: A Christian Foundation for Ethics and Doctrine.*

PREFACE

Alternative Futures for Worship is not a product. It is rather a window through which a relationship may be observed. Or to change the image, it is a listening device with which a conversation may be overheard. The participants are sacramental theology, liturgical experience, and the human sciences.

All of life—like all the world—has the possibility of mediating the transformative encounter between God and human history. That is its sacramental character. In the Roman Catholic tradition there has evolved over a long history a system of seven sacraments. These are not our only sacramental experiences. But they occupy a privileged sacramental role in the life of this Christian community.

Each sacrament concerns itself with the religious meanings of some important slice of human life. There are not many slices of life whose patterns and interpreted meanings have not been probed and described by the human sciences. It is crucial, therefore, that sacramental and liturgical theology pay very careful attention indeed to the deliverances of the human sciences. Religious experience cannot, of course, be reduced to the descriptive reports of the human sciences. Yet it would be foolhardy to theologize or "liturgize" apart from serious consideration of these many empirical attempts to understand the character of lived experience in our culture and our time.

Each volume in this series exemplifies the processes of encounter between sacrament, liturgy, and the human sciences: what reports from the human sciences are being considered; how do these understandings affect the meaning structure of the sacrament; how would these meanings find liturgical expression. Every volume in the series has this fundamental agenda, but each takes it up in its own particular way. Our aims are modest; we have not intended to produce any exactly right conclusion. We only care to engage in serious, imaginative, and highly responsible conversation.

It may seem that proposing alternative sacramental rituals is irresponsible, and it would be if they were proposed for anyone's actual use. They are not! This is not an underground sacramentary. We are most aware of the tentative and groping character of each of these attempts.

However, we believe with William James that the best way to understand what something means (like this conversation between Christian experience and the human sciences) is to see what difference it makes. James says you must set an idea to work in the stream of experience to know what it means. We choose ritual as that stream of experience.

Sacramental rituals are not themselves the sacraments. The sacraments are temporally thick slices of life which through time mediate religious experience. The liturgical rite is but one moment in this thicker-than-rite sacramentalization of life. It is a privileged moment though. Ritual is a moment of high value if it illuminates and intensifies the meaning of sacrament. Leonard Bernstein's "Mass for Theatre" speaks movingly of the absurdity of ritual when it has lost touch with the lives of the people who are supposed to be celebrating it. When private meanings and public ritual meanings do not intersect (which is not to say coincide), the absurdity is thundering.

Because a ritual puts a sacramental understanding under the spotlight, we have elected to explore the conversation between sacramental life and the human sciences by imagining ritual appropriations of the fruits of the conversation. That is our way of setting an idea to work imaginatively in the stream of experience. That, and nothing more! But that is a lot.

We suggest that any readers of this volume who have not done so read the introductory volume. There we have tried to say more fully what we think we are about in this entire series and why the many authors who contributed to it are convinced that this project is a quite right thing to do. We are happy to have you listen in on our conversation. Our long-term hope is that you may join it.

Bernard Lee, S.M.
San Antonio, Texas

INTRODUCTION

Mark Searle

Process is a key term in this whole project of exploring *Alternative Futures for Worship,* and no single sacrament is as calculated to demonstrate the importance of process in the Christian life as is the sacrament of baptism. Perhaps we should say the *sacraments* of baptism; for baptism is the general name from early Christian tradition for the whole complex of initiation rites which brought and still brings new members into the life of the Church and into the Body of Christ. That complex of rites culminates in the Easter sacraments of baptism, confirmation, and Eucharist, but the culminating ritual event is both the summit of all that has gone before to initiate newcomers to Christianity and the source of a lifelong process, or "journey of faith," which is not over until sacramental shadows yield to the bright vision of God.

Thus, while the process character of other sacramental rites has become obscured with the passage of time, the process character of Christian initiation has never entirely been eclipsed. It did, however, suffer some distortion as catechesis became separated from ritual initiation, and the culminating sacramental celebration fell apart into distinct sacramental events, often celebrated years apart from each other. One of the significant achievements of contemporary Christianity has been the recognition that the sacraments of baptism, confirmation, and Eucharist belong together and together they belong to a larger initiatory process. Hence has come the promulgation of the *Rite for the Christian Initiation of Adults* (1972) in the Roman Catholic Church and the tentative development of similar guidelines for the initiation of adults and older children in other Churches in the West.

Precisely because the Churches in recovering their tradition have already opened up a new and exciting future for adult initiation—one based precisely on the recognition of the process character of conversion and initiation—it seems more valuable to look at the initiation of infants and young children. Here the process of pregnancy, birthing, homecoming, parenting, and growth is seen as a complex flow of lives interacting upon each other, where past experiences are reconfigured and new possibilities open up to shape the future, not only for the child but for all those touched by the arrival of the child. Since grace does not operate apart from such fluctuating relationships but gives ultimate meaning to them all—the gracious presence and redemptive love of God's own Spirit—the whole process is broadly sacramental, summed up, interpreted, and celebrated in the faith celebrations and sacramental rites of the believing community. Thus the focus of this initiation volume in the series *Alternative Futures for Worship* will restrict itself to the exploration of infant initiation. Further it will be assumed for the purposes of the exercise that such sacramental initiation of infants will comprise baptism, confirmation, and Eucharist celebrated in the course of a single, unitary liturgy.[1]

In chapter 1 Mark Searle reexamines both the practice of infant initiation in the West and the arguments for and against it, suggesting that the time has come to look at the Church's ancient practice in entirely new ways. The groundwork for a new approach to the understanding and practice of infant baptism is laid in chapter 2 with Andrew Thompson's comprehensive survey of research in the social sciences into the place of the child in the family system and the influence of the configuration of the family upon the developing personality of the child. Methodologically this is the cornerstone of the volume, since all the other writers take Thompson's chapter as their starting point. Thus Herbert Anderson in chapter 3 begins to translate the kind of insights offered by Thompson into pastoral strategy for the Church in its care of the family and especially in its care of the family before, during, and after the birth of a new child. Such events, lived in faith, must make a difference to the way faith is not only understood but celebrated ritually. Insights into the process of pregnancy, birth, and parenthood derived from the social sciences should make a difference in the way we understand the workings of grace and in the way we ritualize the grace dimension of those events. Hence in chapter 4, Gail Ramshaw-Schmidt offers a proposal for celebrating the initiation of infants in stages. This proposal is respectfully offered to the Churches, not so much for direct implementation, but as a stimulus to a more thoroughgoing reappraisal of present practices and the development of an order of infant initiation as radical and as serious as that developed for adult initiation. Finally two theologians reflect on the whole enterprise. In chapter 5 Robert Duggan reflects on the implications of this approach for adult initiation, while in chapter 6 Stephen Happel looks at some methodological issues involved in using the social sciences in sacramental theology and pastoral liturgy.

In the very nature of things, no process is ever complete unless it be taken up into some further process. So it is here. What has been begun needs to be taken further, beyond the first weeks and months of life into the broader stream of sacramental processes in the ongoing life of the Church. The same must be said of the tentative pastoral and theological ideas launched in this volume. The authors will be well satisfied if their work contributes to ongoing critical reflection on the sacramental and pastoral practice of the Churches.

Footnote

1. This was, of course, the practice of the universal Church for the first millenium and remains the practice of the Eastern Churches. In the West there is growing ecumenical consensus that if infants are fit subjects for baptism, they are also fit subjects for chrismation and the Eucharist. See, for example, *". . . and do not hinder them." An Ecumenical Plan for the Admission of Children to the Eucharist.* Faith and Order Paper no. 109, ed. G. Müller-Fahrenholz (Geneva: World Council of Churches, 1982). Also *Nurturing Children in Communion*, ed. Colin Buchanon, Grove Liturgical Studies, n. 44 (Bramcote, Notts. 1985). Several Churches in the United States (Lutheran, Episcopalian, Methodist) have restored chrismation to infant baptism and left confirmation as a nonsacramental, repeatable public profession of faith.

1. INFANT BAPTISM RECONSIDERED

Mark Searle

"What the value of baptizing infants might be is an extremely obscure question. But one must believe there is some value in it."
St. Augustine. *De quantitate animae*, XXXVI, 80.

During the past twenty or thirty years sacramental theology has undergone an enormous transformation. Undoubtedly the leading indicator if not the cause of this transformation is the abandonment of the questions and vocabulary of Scholasticism in favor of more existentialist and personalist approaches to understanding what sacraments are and how they function in the Christian life. What began as a recovery of the ecclesial dimension of the sacraments quickly led to further shifts: from speaking of sacraments as "means of grace" to speaking of them as encounters with Christ himself; from thinking of them primarily as acts of God to thinking of them mainly as celebrations of the faith community; from seeing sacraments as momentary incursions from another world to seeing them as manifestations of the graced character of all human life; from interpreting them as remedies for sin and weakness to seeing them as promoting growth in Christ.

Such shifts have been prompted in part by theological developments but also by the influence, both on theology and pastoral practice, of a growing awareness of the radically altered sociocultural circumstances in which the Christian life is lived in the second half of the twentieth century. Yet while the practice of infant baptism has been particularly challenged in this "post-Christian" era, it has remained strangely neglected in the work of theological reconstruction. Instead, theological discussion of infant baptism remains largely dominated by the inherited methodologies of historical study and deductive arguments from doctrinal first principles.

Yet infant initiation is deserving of more imaginative reconsideration. It remains an issue close to the experience of every believing family. But even from the theologian's perspective, if most of the issues of current theological interest come together in the sacraments,[1] most sacramental questions come together in a particularly concentrated way in the issue of the sacramental initiation of infants. Here converge such problems as how to speak of God, the relationship between the order of grace and the order of history, the relationship between grace and freedom, the nature and role of the Church as mediating the mystery of salvation, and the relationship between the language of faith and the basic experiences of human life. Conversely, of course, one's personal and denominational position on such issues as these will invariably color one's understanding of what, if anything, is transpiring when an infant is baptized.

The focus of this chapter, however, will be considerably more modest. Less than a theology of infant initiation, this will be more of a prolegomenon for such a theology, looking at how the question of infant baptism has been raised in the past, how it poses itself today, and how it might be approached differently in order to break out of the stalemate to which traditional arguments have led. In this way, it is hoped, this chapter will prepare the ground for the later contributions of this volume.

Notes for a History of the Question

History shows for the most part that where the sacraments are concerned, practice is invariably a step or two ahead of theology. With the exception of the Reformation, the practice of baptism gives rise to theological reflection rather than being shaped by a priori theological principles. Thus it is necessary to distinguish between the practice of infant baptism and theological attempts either to justify it, to undermine it, or to influence the shape of its practice. Similarly there are two distinct if related histories: the history of the practice of infant baptism and the history of its theology. Here it is clearly impossible to give an adequate account of either history, so we shall be content to make some observations on each with a view to demonstrating the need for a fresh look at the whole matter.

On the History of Baptism

In most accounts of the history of infant initiation, too little consideration has been given to the relationship between infant baptism and clinical or deathbed baptism. The question of whether the early Church baptized has been debated to a standstill.[2] The evidence is insufficient to draw any firm conclusions either way, though in the final analysis what we know about familial unity and patriarchal authority in the ancient world makes it less than likely that the children of Christian parents would have been left to make a decision for themselves. The apparently fairly widespread practice of deferring baptism until rather late in life would seem to be a secondary development of the fourth century associated with the discipline of once-in-a-lifetime penance. What we do know with complete certitude, however, is that infants who were baptized (and the evidence becomes universal after the year 200) were initiated along with adult converts in the paschal sacraments of water, chrism, and altar.

The fact that infants and young children were wholly initiated needs to be underlined, because the subsequent breakup of Christian initiation into distinct celebrations of infant baptism, delayed confirmation, and separate "first Communion" was never something deliberately chosen or decided by the Church. It just happened. It happened despite the best efforts of Church authorities from late antiquity to the High Middle Ages to prevent it happening and to mitigate its effects. The ideal of unified sacramental initiation for infants and young children remains in place in the East and in some parts of Hispanic Catholicism. In most of the West, however, the postponement of episcopal confirmation lasted so long, despite efforts to avoid it, that it came to be accepted first as inevitable and eventually as desirable. Apparently resigning themselves to the disintegration of the rites of initiation, the Churches of the West came increasingly to endorse the separation of confirmation and first Communion from baptism, though it only became a universal policy after the Council of Trent.[3]

The root causes of this drift towards separation are to be found as far back as the third century in provisions made for the baptizing of catechumens in danger of death. The fourth-century Church historian Eusebius cites the comments of Pope Cornelius († 253) on the sad history of the heretic Novatian. The pope ascribed Novatian's defection from the unity of the Church of Rome to the fact that he had been baptized in an emergency when he had fallen seriously ill and was thought to be near death. When subsequently he recovered, he allegedly never went to the bishop for the completion of the rites of initiation: "Without receiving these, how could he receive the Holy Spirit?"[4]

Whatever the facts of Novatian's case, the practice of baptizing catechumens thought to be on the point of death and the subsequent completion of their initiation by the bishop if they recovered are clearly attested in the following period. Thus the Council of Elvira, Spain, in 305 ordained as follows:

> Canon 38: *That in cases of necessity even laypersons* [fideles] *may baptize.*
>> It was agreed that a faithful man who has held fast to his baptism and is not bigamous may baptize a sick catechumen at sea, or wherever there is no church at hand, provided that if he survives he shall bring him to a bishop so that he may be confirmed [*perfici*] through the laying-on of a hand.[5]

Presumably the same held true for infants who were born sickly and considered unlikely to survive. Normally children would be kept for baptism at Easter, to be initiated along with the rest of the catechumens, but if their life was in danger they would, like any other catechumen in danger of death, be baptized without delay and would have their initiation completed by the bishop if and when they recovered.

But what had at first been the exceptional case eventually became commonplace as an increasing percentage of the candidates for baptism came in fact to be children in a period where infancy was itself so precarious a condition that to be newborn was ipso facto to be in a life-threatening situation. Even without the additional encouragement of the Augustinian doctrine of the damnation of unbaptized infants, it is hard to imagine that emergency baptisms would not have been more common in the fifth and sixth centuries simply because baptismal candidates were predominantly children and because of the high incidence of infant mortality. Surviving documentary evidence would seem to support this hypothesis. Although the eighth-century supplement to the *Hadrianum* contained a form of catechumenate and initiation liturgy suitably abbreviated for infants, it is significant that this did not apparently catch on. Instead, infant baptism was increasingly celebrated using the much older Gelasian *Order for the Making of a Catechumen or for Baptizing.* But this rite was nothing other than a rite for baptizing the dying! So common did its use become in the Middle Ages that it eventually came to serve as the basis for the rite of infant baptism in the Roman Ritual of 1614.[6]

Thus it seems obvious that *quamprimum* infant baptism was simply a form of clinical baptism. Much later on, the Council of Florence implicitly admitted as much in its decree of 1442:

> Concerning children: because of the danger of death, which occurs frequently enough, since nothing else can be done for them except to baptize them, whereby they are snatched from the power of the devil and adopted as children of God, the Council admonishes that holy baptism is not to be delayed for 40 or 80 days or for some other period of time, as some are wont to do, but they should be baptized as soon as conveniently possible [*quamprimum commode fieri potest*]. Therefore, in imminent danger of death, let them be baptized in the form of the Church even by a layman or woman, if no priest is at hand, quickly and without delay.[7]

What came to differentiate the situation of infants from that of unbaptized adults who fell gravely ill was that in the course of time, beginning in the late thirteenth century, the subsequent completion of their initiation came deliberately to be postponed until they had reached the "age of discretion," if indeed they lived that long.[8] Slowly and imperceptibly the Church had completed a volte-face, gradually abandoning its insistence that surviving children be brought to the bishop as soon as possible after baptism and suggesting instead that confirmation be "prudently" delayed until the children were old enough to need the sacrament.

The facts of the story are well enough known. What is not always recognized is that with this unwitting change of policy, the Western Church gave up trying to initiate infants. Once infant baptism is recognized as a form of clinical baptism—an emergency measure—it has to be acknowledged that, with the move to defer confirmation and first Communion, Christian initiation was in fact deferred until the child was old enough to be catechized. Instead of initiating infants, as had been the universal policy of the first millennium or more, the Church now put them on hold—baptizing them as a precautionary measure—until they came of age. The Catechism of the Council of Trent endorsed this deferred initiation for the Roman Church when it described the administration of confirmation to children under seven as "inexpedient" and went on to say: "Wherefore, if not to be postponed to the age of twelve, it is most proper to defer this sacrament at least to that of seven."[9]

What made this change of direction thinkable, of course, was the new theology of confirmation as a distinct sacrament, which the early medieval theologians had elaborated in an effort to persuade parents to bring their children to the bishop for the completion of their initiation. As it happens, the rationale for receiving the sacrament eventually became a rationale for delaying it until the age of seven, the age at which for many purposes a child ceased to be regarded as a child and was numbered among the company of adults.[10] The net result is that, beginning in the late thirteenth century and universally from the sixteenth, the Roman Catholic Church has really only initiated "adults," even though it continued to baptize the newborn as a precautionary measure within a few hours or days of birth. There is an irony here not often remarked upon: Roman Catholics and Anabaptists were actually closer together in their positions on infant baptism than they thought. Recognizing the precautionary and emergency character of infant baptism in the Roman Church does go a long way towards accounting for the largely remedial attitude towards baptism in post-Tridentine theology, as well as for the emphasis on catechesis as a necessary precondition for being confirmed and for making one's first confession and first Communion.

Since it is only in the twentieth century that the full history of the practice of initiation in the West has become available, such developments as we have described occurred without much sense of anyone introducing radical change. With that history now available, however, the Church is for the first time in a position to ask the question of whether the "accidental" reversal of her original policy with regard to the initiation of children is something she still wants to endorse. But since there is no virtue in returning to an earlier practice simply because it was earlier, such a decision will require serious reflection on the place of the child in the economy of grace.

On the History of Baptismal Theology

Here again we shall confine ourselves to some remarks about the way the question of infant baptism has been posed at certain key moments in its history, with a particular eye to seeing whether the child as such was ever taken into account.

The New Testament and the Subapostolic Church

There is little or no evidence that infant baptism was ever posed as a question, unless Luke 18:15-17 be read that way.[11] Though some, such as Kurt Aland,[12] would take the silence of the first two centuries as indicating that the Church did not baptize infants, it is more likely, for the reason mentioned above, that the inclusion of infants and small children among the ranks of the baptizands was simply taken for granted. Moreover it should also be noted that children are among the beneficiaries of Jesus' miraculous cures in the Gospels, and that when they are mentioned at all in the teaching of Jesus it is to hold them up as paradigms of those who receive or are received into the Kingdom of God (see Mark 10:14-15; Luke 9:47-48; 18:15-17; Matt 18:1-5; 19:13-15). Thus while there is nothing directly excluding the baptism of children, children are put in a very positive light where the appropriation of salvation is concerned, a fact all the more remarkable in view of the predominantly negative view of children which subsequently came to prevail in the West.

Tertullian (North Africa, c. 150–220)

Tertullian is the first writer known to have challenged the practice of baptizing infants and children.[13] It is notable that he neither challenges the validity of such baptisms nor questions the authenticity of the practice as an apostolic tradition. Instead he is content merely to argue that it is unnecessary and unwise. It is unnecessary, he says, because children have committed no sins—"why should innocent infancy come with haste to the remission of sins?" Yet elsewhere Tertullian seems firmly convinced that every child born into this world is born as a child of Adam and subject to Satan's dominion.[14] The baptism of children is also unwise, for it involves a double jeopardy: jeopardy for the baptized themselves, if they grow up unfaithful to their baptism, and jeopardy for their sponsors, who may be prevented by death from fulfilling their commitment or may be thwarted by the child growing up with "an evil disposition." It is far wiser, Tertullian argues, to "let them be made Christians when they have become competent to know Christ." That competence means more than attaining catechizable age is clear from his advice in the same context that the unmarried should also defer baptism until such time as they have settled down either to marriage or to a life of continence.

What seems to be operative behind these suggestions is Tertullian's view of the *sacramentum* as a sacred oath of commitment and of the Church as a community of the vowed.[15] "All who understand what a burden baptism is will have more fear of obtaining it than of its postponement."[16] Thus for Tertullian baptism is a covenantal relationship in which both God and the baptized have reciprocal responsibilities, responsibilities which a child should not assume (apart presumably from imminent danger of death), because the risk of postbaptismal sin is too great. While Tertullian is the only author on record to have stated this position so clearly, the tendency to defer baptism, which becomes widespread in the fourth century, indicates that his views came to be widely shared.

Augustine (North Africa, 354-430)

The major contributor to a theology of sacraments in the West was Augustine, and nowhere was his influence more keenly felt than in the area of infant baptism. At a time when Christian parents frequently enrolled their children as catechumens but postponed their baptism indefinitely while their children were healthy, Augustine provided a major impetus towards quamprimum baptism.[17] Against the Pelagian emphasis on human responsibility in the work of salvation, Augustine stressed the absolute necessity of the grace of Christ. What was at issue was not the baptism of infants as such but the significance of the redemptive work of Christ in human history and in the life of each individual. Infants became a test case, and Augustine was able to point to the Church's traditional practice of baptizing even newborn children with the "one baptism for the forgiveness of sins" as evidence that they, too, were in sin and in need of Christ's saving grace.

Yet Augustine's autobiographical Confessions reveal a profound ambivalence in his attitude towards children and childhood.[18] On the one hand there is his extraordinary journey back into his own childhood, where he finds the roots of his later sins in the anxious grasping of the child, which he identifies as concupiscence. On the other hand when he begins to speak of his conversion, it is to childhood that he again returns for images of what the truly converted experience. Margaret Miles summarizes Augustine as follows:

> The imagery with which he introduces the conversion experience is that of the child just learning to walk: "Throw yourself on him. Do not fear. He will not pull away and let you fall. Throw yourself without fear and he will receive you and heal you" (Confessions, VIII:1). This strong imagery suggests, as do several other elements in the account, that what is necessary is a return to the earliest psychic condition of anxiety, a stripping of the cumulative object-orientation which, in adulthood, has become ingrained behavior.[19]

The ambivalence of Augustine's imagery is reflective of the ambivalence of the child. On the one hand childhood is the primordial experience of the dialectic between dependence and autonomy, grasping and letting go, to which true conversion must return and which it must redeem through reliving this dialectic under the influence of grace. In that sense childhood is an ideal state to be recovered, not just a past to be left behind. On the other hand since the child unconsciously seeks to resolve its anxiety by reaching and grasping and demanding, the root of all sin, concupiscence, is vividly displayed in its crying and its orality. As such the child represents all that is wrong with fallen humanity: "Who would not tremble and wish rather to die than to be an infant again if the choice were put before him?"[20]

In subsequent Western theology it was the darker side of the child, accentuated in Augustine's anti-Pelagian writings, which seems to have come to dominate. In the ninth century Walafrid Strabo reversed Augustine's argument: "Since all who are not delivered by God's grace will perish in original sin, including those who have not added to it by their own personal sin, it is necessary to baptize infants."[21] Thereafter the practice of infant baptism will be justified on the basis of the doctrine of original sin, not vice versa, and the negative view of childhood will prevail until modern times.

The High Middle Ages: the Eleventh to the Thirteenth Centuries

This period witnessed a resurgence of Manichean dualism, which saw the world of material creation as diametrically opposed to the world of the spirit and as the creation of the Evil One. This resurgence, occurring in the context of demands for Church reform and a return to the simplicity and purity of the Gospel, was often marked by a literal interpretation of the Scriptures. One such instance was the repudiation by the Cathars of infant baptism. As part of their argument, they cited Mark 16:16: "Whosoever believes and is baptized shall be saved and whosoever refuses belief shall be condemned." This challenged orthodox theologians to find ways of justifying the traditional doctrine that infants were saved by baptism even though they were clearly incapable of believing.

One answer was to distinguish between faith as an act of belief and faith as the habitual capacity for making such acts. "The infant," wrote Peter of Poitiers, "can neither believe, nor hope, nor love; yet it has faith, hope and love, just as it is endowed with reason even though it cannot yet reason and has the capacity for laughter even though it cannot yet laugh."[22] St. Thomas Aquinas would make the same point, while adopting Plato's dubious analogy with the sleeping adult: "The inability of the child to act results not from the lack of the *habitus*, but from bodily incapacity, just as people who are asleep are prevented by sleep from exercising the virtues even though they do have the *habitus* of the virtues."[23] So infants are suitable subjects for baptism, the sacrament of faith, because despite their natural incapacity they receive the infused virtue of faith—together with hope and love—through the sacrament itself. Here, clearly, the Augustinian view of the child as equipped with an active if perverted will is temporarily eclipsed by a view of childhood centered on its dormant rationality. The child is the passive recipient of the ministrations of the Church as it is the passive recipient of the ministrations of its own parents, at least until its latent rational powers begin to stir.

The Sixteenth-Century Reformation

Since the key issue of the Reformation was justification, and since the Reformers generally accentuated the role of faith in the Christian life, it was hardly surprising that infant baptism became an issue. For Martin Luther the sacraments were quite secondary to faith in the divine promises, of whose reality they were tangible evidence, but it was a relatively small faction of the Reformers who took this doctrine to its logical conclusion. The Anabaptists, who derived their nickname from their refusal to recognize the validity of infant baptism and their insistence on rebaptizing those baptized in infancy, held that God's grace came through his Word and that baptism only had value for someone who submitted to baptism as an act of submission to the Gospel.

While the Anabaptists represented a number of divergent views, they were generally of one mind in seeing baptism as a personal response to the Word of God, whereby a person covenants with other converted Christians to become the Church, the witnessing community. Since children are inherently incapable of such response or responsibility, they are incapable of baptism. The problem of original sin was resolved largely by ignoring it, since it was not clearly taught in Scripture.

Behind this Anabaptist approach to baptism, as behind much of the reforming program of both the Protestant Reformation and the Catholic Reformation, was the emerging modern concept of the person as an autonomous individual.[24] Whereas earlier and non-

Western concepts of the person tended to identify the person in terms of his or her place in the community, the modern concept of the autonomous individual makes the individual self the source of its values and its own identity. Hence we have the emphasis on individual conversion and commitment and on the education which would shape each individual to take his place in the Church or in society. Through diligent training of intellect and will, Catholics and Protestants alike believed, a new generation of committed individuals could be formed. The Anabaptists in a sense set the pace for the other Churches in the sixteenth century by taking the logical step of deferring baptism until the child's education—the training of intellect, will, and conscience—had been completed, and a full, conscious, and deliberate act of obedience to the Gospel could be made. "This emphasis on personal, individually-sought baptism, exclusive of the religious community into which one entered at birth, earmarked Swiss, Dutch and German Anabaptists alike."[25]

Both Martin Luther and John Calvin rejected the Anabaptist position and retained the practice of baptizing infants, each of them for reasons that had little to do with baptism as such and still less to do with any sympathetic understanding of childhood.[26] Yet the same trend, symptomatic of the new humanism of the age, manifested itself in these other Churches as well, even though for various reasons its complete logical expression, denial of baptism to children, was inhibited. In a direct response to the dilemma raised by the Anabaptists, the other Protestant Churches reinterpreted confirmation—which they regarded not as a sacrament but as an ecclesiastical institution—as a rite of personal profession (confirmation) of faith which concluded the catechizing of those baptized in infancy.

The conservative defensiveness of the Roman Church towards everything suggested or promoted by the Reformers strongly mitigated the influence of this focus on the individual, but one symptom of it that does appear is the definitive move to postpone confirmation and first Communion, if not until the age of twelve then at least until the child reached the age of intellectual and moral discretion. The child might continue to be baptized in the faith of the Church, but the fullness of sacramental initiation would have to wait until the child was old enough to profess its own faith.

Implicit in this position is the identification of Christian life with adult life and with *individual* adult life. Until such time as they develop such adult capacities as intellect, will, and conscience, children can have no real place in the Church; they are barred from the sacraments. Childhood is seen merely as a period between birth and personhood. Not much more can be said for it than that it will pass.

The Twentieth Century

Modern discussions of infant baptism have been largely stimulated by a growing sense of the fragility of Christianity in the modern Western world and by the perceived need for a more credible witness to the Gospel in contemporary society. At first the discussion tended to focus among Protestants on whether the New Testament and the historical tradition offered any legitimation for the practice of infant baptism, but soon the argument shifted to more explicitly doctrinal positions.[27] What was ultimately at stake was less the salvation of infants (for the doctrine of original sin in its Augustinian formulation had been considerably diluted in the course of the nineteenth century) than the salvation of the Church as a witnessing community. The indiscriminate practice of baptizing any child presented at the font was agreed by all to be detrimental. What was at issue was whether infant baptism as such was an apostolic practice compatible with the Gospel or whether it was a later practice symptomatic of a loss of evangelical consciousness.

Among Roman Catholics the legitimacy and validity of infant baptism was never called into question, but in the de-Christianized conditions of postwar Europe, the Catholic Church faced the problems of a vast nominal membership and few deeply committed Catholics. Moves to curtail indiscriminate baptism were accompanied on the one hand by a recovery of the rich patristic teachings on sacramental initiation and on the other hand by the first steps towards a restoration of the ancient catechumenate.[28] In America these issues were taken up after the Second Vatican Council and especially in the wake of the promulgation of the *Rite for the Christian Initiation of Adults*.[29] As the name indicates, this was not exactly a full restoration of the baptismal discipline of the patristic Church, since it was now reserved for adults and for children of catechizable age. Younger children, who had taken their place alongside their elders in the original catechumenate, were henceforth excluded. For them a separate rite was provided, the *Ordo Baptizandi Parvulos* (1969).

This two-fold economy of sacramental initiation has not taken care of the issue of infant baptism, however. In fact it has served to raise new theological problems about what we are doing in baptizing small children.[30] Nor are these problems confined to discussions among academic theologians, for the contrast between the extensiveness and symbolic richness of the adult rite and the relatively perfunctory character of the children's rite, both witnessed in the same parishes, has raised questions for pastors and faithful as well. Since this is where matters currently stand, it is worth identifying some of the challenges posed to infant baptism by the RCIA more closely.

Infant Baptism in the Shadow of the RCIA

There has been a tendency since the elaboration of the scholastic synthesis of sacramental theology in the thirteenth century to focus on the individual minister and recipient at the expense of the ecclesial context, on the sacramental moment at the expense of the initiatory process, on the efficacy of the sacramental act at the expense of the role of faith, and on the remedial value of baptism at the expense of the rich symbolism of the unified rites of baptism, confirmation, and Eucharist. On all these counts the RCIA brings welcome redress, but in doing so it calls into question the strategy of infant baptism whose ritual remains comparatively impoverished. The newly restored practice of adult initiation serves to highlight precisely those aspects of baptismal theology which the new rite of infant baptism continues to obscure. We shall identify four such elements, four elements with which any rethinking of infant baptism will require us to come to terms.

The Faith of the Candidate

In contrast to the passivity of the infant, the adult coming to baptism is capable of faith and of all that faith implies. He or she can play a full, conscious, and active role in responding to the call of God's Word and submitting to the power of God's grace.

This powerful event of adult conversion has traditionally been envisaged in America in one of two ways. First, there is the early Anabaptist tradition, maintained by present-day Mennonites and some Baptists, for which this coming to faith is essentially cognitive and the product of conviction: a submission to the judgment of God's Word upon one's life and upon the world. It issues in a life-style which takes the Gospel seriously and glories in its countercultural challenge. Such conversion is radical, evangelical, and ethical. But there is another more widespread and certainly more recent tradition among American Protestant fundamentalists, in which conversion is less a matter of conviction than of experience. Here baptism itself is subordinated to the "amazing grace" of discovering Jesus as one's personal savior.

These two traditions of adult conversion—the one issuing in a common life of evangelical discipleship, the other in a more individualistic, feeling experience of "being saved"—have both had some influence on American Roman Catholics as they adopt the RCIA. The effect of both is to render infant baptism an anomaly, and if Roman Catholics have shown themselves hesitant to rule out infant baptism altogether, they have certainly begun to raise questions about its value. These two native American conceptions of conversion come together with a traditional Catholic emphasis on faith as belief, to make conversion a highly personal decision and the celebration of baptism the occasion of a maturely considered faith commitment. It thereby achieves successfully what Catholics have been trying to do with confirmation with far less effect. The problem of "what to do with confirmation" is itself a trailing symptom, some would argue, of the problem created by infant baptism: membership in the Church without any guarantee that those so baptized will ever come to own their baptismal faith.

The Ecclesiological Factor

As in the past, so too in the present, a preference for adult over infant baptism is closely tied to a particular ecclesiology. This connection is sometimes explicit, as with the Anabaptists and Mennonites, but it often lurks behind the screen of other arguments, as was the case with Tertullian. Today in the Roman Catholic Church, as in previous eras of reform, there is something of a reaction against the Church's perceived cultural compromises and the dream of a more faithful if smaller Church. Instead of the security and blandness of the *Volkskirche*, some hope for a believers' Church: a Church of small base communities whose members are committed to working in the world with uncompromising fidelity to Gospel values. Since Karl Rahner, Catholics have been accustomed to refer to this as the "diaspora Church." It envisages a fully active membership, gathered in small congregations, which will be fully participatory in their polity and marked by an evangelical life-style. Priority will be given to local congregations and to their self-discipline within the larger communion of the Church as a whole, rather than to the large, amorphous entities represented by national and international religious denominations. The dream of many contemporary Catholics could be summed up as "solidarity without legalism and pastoral responsibility without clericalism."

Among Avery Dulles' five models of Church,[31] this one obviously corresponds most closely to the "Herald" model, with strong overtones of the "Servant" model, but it is interesting to note that Catholics often appeal in support of such a vision to conciliar texts such as *Sacrosanctum Concilium* #41 and *Lumen Gentium* #26. Here the Church is said to manifest itself most adequately and visibly in the local assembly, where the faithful gather under the presidency of the bishop for the celebration of the liturgy. In appealing to these texts, it is not always recognized that two quite different models of Church are being fused. While this is of itself quite legitimate, the debate over infant baptism is muddied by the failure to acknowledge the new hybrid ecclesiology and to work out the implications of clinging to the sacramental model of Church while opting to develop a form of Church organization on the herald model. The Anabaptists in adopting the herald model rejected sacramentalism. Catholics appear as yet unwilling to face the issue: can a congregational model of Church with its emphasis upon the Word of God and on the need for adult decision be reconciled with the Catholic sacramental tradition, with its faith in the power of grace to work below the level of consciousness, even in the baptism of a child?

New Understanding of Sacramentality

One of the major contributions of the RCIA to Catholic life and to sacramental theology is the way in which it has forced us to break with an almost magical understanding of the sacraments as discrete moments of divine intervention and to adopt a more flexible understanding of sacramentality as a process admitting of degrees. In this latter perspective the temporal duration of the catechumenal process, the various stages in the journey of faith undertaken by the candidates, the various ritual celebrations that mark the way culminating in the solemn Easter rites of baptism, confirmation, and Eucharist are all sacramental in varying degrees. The liturgy of Easter night is less the setting for three discrete sacramental "moments" than it is the climax of a process which is sacramental in its entirety.

The concept of a gradual growth in faith, marked by a succession of rites and stages which are themselves sacramental in a broad sense, offers an obviously attractive solution to the problem of infant baptism.[32] By enrolling infants in the catechumenate, we can give them something, whether their parents are committed Christians or not, while still withholding baptism until the children are old enough to ask for it themselves and to make a lasting commitment. There is obviously a precedent for such an arrangement in the Church of the fourth and fifth centuries.

What is remarkable in most of the discussion of the proposed infant catechumenate, however, is that two points are rarely, if ever, addressed. First, the rite of enrollment in the catechumenate requires of candidates that they already have manifested some initial conversion and that they be prepared to make their intentions known to the Church.[33] Second, the issue of when a child would be old enough to be elected for baptism is rarely indicated. Would it be at the age of three, as Gregory Nazianzen suggested in the fourth century, when the child is old enough to remember its baptism? Would it be a year or two after the child is old enough to be catechized? Or would baptism be witheld until the child is old enough to make a mature personal decision? Any solution but the latter—which would perhaps delay baptism until the child was of marriageable age—is vulnerable to at least some of the objections raised against infant baptism and would thus constitute only a partial solution.

In actual fact while enrolling the child in the catechumenate is often promoted on the grounds that the rite of enrollment is itself a kind of sacrament, the desire to delay the baptism of children until they are old enough to take part actively in their own initiation is itself associated with a "low" view of sacraments. The deferment of the sacrament makes sense because sacraments are seen more in terms of their nature as human actions than in terms of their nature as acts of God. There is, in other words, a possible inconsistency in subjecting the helpless infant to the "sacramentality" of enrollment in the catechumenate but refusing to submit it to the "sacramentality" of the complete rite of initiation.

The Meaning of Baptism

For centuries, as we saw, popular Catholic understanding of baptism was dominated by Augustine's teaching that children dying in original sin would be excluded forever from the vision of God. Conciliar teaching on the Christian life and the renewed rites of Christian initiation have shifted attention to the more positive aspects of baptism and especially to the paschal character of the Christian life as a sharing in the death and resurrection of Christ.

This is an immense gain, but the paschal character of baptism is sometimes propounded in such a way as to seem to preclude the baptism of infants. When Aidan Kavanagh, for example, describes baptism as "a transitus from shame to celebration, from the conviction of sin to the appropriation of one's complete forgiveness in Christ"[34] little room appears left for the baptizing of preconscious infants.

With respect to this emphasis on the radical discontinuity between the "before" and "after" of baptism, two points need to be made. The first is that studies on the meaning of *pascha* in Christian usage have shown that it was used in three distinct if related senses and that the translation *pascha = transitus* (transition, journey) is relatively late and only became widespread with Augustine.[35] The popularity of the *transitus* meaning and its eclipse of the earlier meanings (which interpreted the term as referring either to God passing over the children of Israel and sparing their lives or to the lamb—Christ—by whose blood they were spared) was largely due to the association of adult baptism (passage through the waters) with the Easter Vigil. Thus it is somewhat tautologous to argue that the paschal character of baptism requires the kind of break with the past which characterizes adult conversion, when it was precisely that sort of conversion which led to *pascha* being identified with the people's passage through the Red Sea rather than with God's merciful sparing of his children.

Secondly, research on the early history of Christian baptism, especially in East Syria, has made it abundantly clear that not everything in Christian life can be reduced to the death/resurrection motif and that this was not quite the root metaphor for baptism either in the New Testament or in early Christianity that some have supposed it to be. In fact, for reasons which no one has yet been able to explain, the Pauline doctrine on baptism as a participation in the death and resurrection of Christ was totally without influence in the first three centuries of the Church.[36] Instead, the dominant image, especially in Syria, was not Calvary but the Jordan, not the death of Jesus, but his baptism and manifestation as Son.[37] Around the image of the baptism of Jesus and his messianic anointing being shared by those being baptized, there clustered a whole range of images much more congenial to the baptism of infants: adoption, divinization, sanctification, gift of the Spirit, indwelling, glory, power, wisdom, rebirth, restoration, mission, and so forth. These, it should be noted, are as much part of the traditional meaning of baptism as the death and resurrection imagery. But this is not to suggest that we retain one set of meanings for adult initiation and another set for infant initiation. On the contrary, both sets of images are properly activated in any baptism, which means that adult initiation needs to be thought of in terms of rebirth and return to infancy, while infants, if they are to be baptized, must be capable in some way of dying and rising with Christ.

CONCLUSION

Having selectively reviewed some aspects of the history of baptismal practice and baptismal theology and looked at some of the challenges to infant initiation posed by the restored adult rite, it is now time to try to pull together what we have learned from this review which might suggest that a rethinking of infant initiation is both timely and necessary. Traditional ways of thinking appear inadequate for the following four reasons.

First, it is striking that past and present discussions about infant baptism are rarely about baptism alone or about infants at all. Usually the subject of infant baptism is raised in the context of another argument, whether it be about the nature of the Church as a community of witness or about the relationship of God's grace to human works. John Calvin's position on the baptism of the children of believers, for example, is entirely derived from his conviction concerning the essential unity of the Old and New Covenants, so that what was said of circumcision for the Jews may be said of baptism for Christian children. The traditional arguments for or against infant baptism, then, are characteristically deductive arguments from a priori doctrinal principles in which the nature of childhood itself is rarely made the subject of theological reflection.

Second, the necessity, legitimacy, and advisability of infant baptism have been addressed from many different angles. The question has been posed in historical terms (did the primitive Church baptize infants?), in pastoral terms (is baptizing people in infancy the best way to socialize them?), in ecclesiological terms (is the Church intended by Christ one that requires adult commitment?) and in sacramental terms (are the sacraments such that they can be effective without the free and knowing cooperation of the recipient?). But the question has rarely if ever been posed theologically (is there any place in the divine economy for the child as child?) or Christologically (what soteriological value is to be ascribed to the infancy and childhood of Jesus?).

Third, infant baptism tends to be favored by those who see the sacraments primarily in terms of the work of God and to be opposed by those who see the sacraments primarily as divinely instituted ways of responding to God's Word. Thus pedobaptists characteristically justify infant initiation on the grounds that it is prime evidence of God's initiative in human salvation; antipedobaptists see God's merciful initiative as located in his intelligible Word, to which only a conscious and informed mind can offer adequate submission. Thus the arguments for or against infant baptism at a doctrinal level appear to be *au fond* arguments about the relative value of Word and sacrament. Does the Word merely prepare for the sacrament? Does the sacrament merely seal our acceptance of the Word in faith? Is baptism the beginning and precondition of further Christian socialization, or is it its crowning moment? Once again, though, the problem with posing the question in this way is that it still neglects to pay any serious attention to the condition of the child as child. Neither the view of the child as not-yet-adult, nor the view that baptism "infuses" a supernatural habitus of faith, hope, and love into the infant, takes seriously the possibility that the infant might live a life of faith, hope, and love precisely as a child and precisely as a child-in-relationship within the context of its own *ecclesia*, the Christian family.

Fourth, the history of the theology of baptism would seem to corroborate the thesis first put forward by Philippe Ariès, namely that the characteristic attitude of adults towards children until modern times was one of indifference. In his classic work *Centuries of Childhood*, published in 1962, Ariès sets out to refute those pundits who idealize the family life of previous generations while decrying the degeneration of family life in the contemporary world. In this mission Ariès admirably succeeds, painting what must seem to us a shocking portrait of neglect and abuse in the raising of children in the medieval and early modern periods. He concludes that adults, including mothers, were generally ignorant of the inner life of the child and, what is more, indifferent to it. Children under the age of six or seven were not really considered as persons but as subrational and thus subhuman. Ariès, of course, is talking about cultural attitudes and about a culture in which the concepts of childhood and family as we understand them had not yet emerged. This cultural mindset does not preclude genuine instances of love for children, of course, any more than our culture's high valuing of children is able to prevent the continuing abuse and exploitation of children in our own society.

Ariès' study on the medieval and early modern periods finds an echo in Robert Pattison's survey of the place of the child in the literature of classical and late antiquity. He writes:

> Certainly the most striking feature of classical literature's attitude towards children is the thunderous silence that envelopes the idea of childhood, especially when compared to the outpouring of concern and attention recent centuries have produced on the same subject.

"The classical silence does not necessarily indicate indifference," he argues; yet he admits that "Roman infants were largely neglected before they came to a reasonable age . . . . Childhood raised few questions and evoked only the slenderest train of associations. The child may have contained the possibility of perfection, but until the possibility actually bore fruit, he remained subrational and therefore subliterary."[38]

It is really only in the seventeenth and eighteenth centuries that Pattison begins to find the child coming to play a role in English literature, a finding which matches Ariès' claim that it was only at this period that the concept of childhood began to emerge. Before that time and to a very large extent for a long while afterwards, children were usually regarded as defective adults. Infancy and young childhood represented a precarious and insignificant introduction to life which properly began somewhere between the ages of four and seven, when the child—now able to speak, understand, and act—was given more or less complete admission to adult life.

In a more recent study of childrearing in seventeenth-century France, David Hunt has introduced an important qualification to Ariès' thesis. He writes:

> Far from viewing the unfolding of infantile potentials with benign indifference, grownups in that period were deeply disturbed by some aspects of the orality, the obstinacy, and the sexuality of their offspring and made determined efforts to mold or thwart altogether such inclinations.[39]

What this correction to Ariès seems to suggest is what the history of the doctrine of original sin would also seem to indicate: children have either been dismissed as subhuman because subrational and thus ignored, or their wilfulness has been recognized and has come to serve as a hook for the projection of adult fears and fantasies. As we remarked before, it is the latter attitude which seems largely to have prevailed in the West until relatively recent times, making children bear the brunt of adult anxieties about sin and salvation.[40] It is only in the twentieth century that serious studies of childhood have come into their own, but even so serious theological reflection on the matter has hardly begun.[41]

A New Approach to Infant Initiation

There are at least three different angles from which a fresh evaluation of the practice of initiating infants to the Christian life might be approached.

From the perspective of the Church itself, which has to be concerned with the effective socialization of each new generation if it is to survive, the whole issue of what constitutes an effective way of socializing needs to be looked at and the place of sacramental celebrations within such a process needs to be considered.[42] It remains the case that because such socialization is presumed to be parish-based, it is only undertaken with preschoolers at the earliest. The Church apparently has nothing to say to or about young children from the time they are baptized shortly after birth until the time when they are old enough to be enrolled in preschool religious education programs. Thus pastoral practice is at odds with the rhetoric of the Second Vatican Council and of the baptismal liturgy, which speaks of the parents and the family as "the first and foremost educators of their children."[43] Any worthwhile rethinking of the Christian formation of the children of believers will therefore have to take both the children and the family more seriously as active participants in the life of the Church.

This would mean, in turn, that the perspective of the family itself needs to be considered and its experience taken into account. More specifically the Christian family is called to understand the events of its life—especially something as significant as pregnancy and childbirth—in the light of faith and to recognize the birth of each new child not only as a gift of God in some generic sense but as a specific word-event of God addressed to them.

Finally the event of baptism needs to be reflected upon from the child's point of view, once it is admitted that there is such a thing as a child's point of view. This would mean exploring how it can be said that the child *as child* can be said to be delivered from sin, adopted by God, incorporated into Christ, and made a dwelling-place of the Holy Spirit.

Here we shall leave the ecclesiastical angle aside to focus more closely on the family and the child. We shall first explore the implications of a theology of the family as a "domestic church" and then look at the possibility of regarding the child as an active participant in the sacramental process.

The Family as Church

The key to a new understanding of infant baptism is the vision of the family as a domestic church, *ecclesiola in ecclesia,* in virtue both of baptism and of the sacrament of marriage.[44] This means that the family, a communion of life in Christ within the larger communion of the local and universal Church, participates in the mystery of the one Church as a sacrament of Christ and in the threefold operation of the Church's priestly, prophetic, and royal mission. Indeed whatever can be said of the Church as a whole can be said, *mutatis mutandis,* of the Christian family. Where the arrival of a new child and the decision for baptism are concerned, this ecclesial identity of the family suggests the following observations.

a. The family, exercising its prophetic function, has to discern the meaning of pregnancy, childbirth, and parenting, not in general but in terms of the birth of this particular child at this particular time. As Herbert Anderson points out in his chapter in this volume, this is not a cue for mindless romanticizing. Very often feelings about the child are ambivalent, while the emotional and physical costs involved in pregnancy, birth, and childrearing are high, and future prospects may appear daunting. It is, in any case, from the specifics of the event and the actual history of its occurrence that faith will seek to read the merciful will of God, so that the event becomes itself a moment of revelation, a Word of God expressed in the contingencies of family life.

b. The events of conception, pregnancy, birth, and parenthood, read in faith, evoke in turn the priestly function of the domestic church: a priesthood exercised in thanksgiving and intercession certainly but also in the rituals and "sacraments" of family life which include everything from prenatal diet and exercise to the most mundane aspects of caring for the newborn.

c. The word and sacrament encountered and lived in the domestic setting find their fulfillment and their touchstone in the liturgical proclamation and celebration of the local Church, especially in the sacraments of the bath, the oil, and the table. Here the old axiom *sacramenta propter homines* (sacraments are for people) needs to be complemented with the corresponding axiom *sacramenta propter ecclesiam* (sacraments are for the Church). In contrast to the scholastic identification of the purpose of the sacraments as twofold—forgiveness and sanctification—the Second Vatican Council teaches that the sacraments have a triple purpose: to sanctify, to build up the Church, to glorify God (SC, 59). Thus baptism is to be understood as celebrated not only for the recipient but for the benefit of the whole community of faith. Realistically this means that baptism is celebrated not only for the infant but for the parents and siblings and for the parish. This is not to suggest, as sometimes seems to be suggested, that the baptism is *really* for the parents or that infant baptism justifies itself as a "teachable moment" in the life of the parents. In a more profound sense the liturgy of baptism depends for its ability to "translate" the child from outside to inside the Church upon the reconstituting of that Church in the liturgical assembly and particularly upon the reconstituting of the family in its organic unity as an *ecclesiola in ecclesia.* If the child is baptized in the faith of the Church, then the identity of the family as constituted by faith, as itself a sacrament of faith, must be "confected" anew in the process and event of sacramental initiation. In short, the family is part of the sacramental sign of baptism and will be confirmed as such by taking its part in the enactment of the rites themselves.[45]

d. The family-as-Church is probably the best context, too, in which to address the issue of what it means to say that baptism is for the forgiveness of sins, or that baptism "washes away" original sin. A major problem with much discussion of the doctrine of original sin is that it is not always sufficiently acknowledged that the concept of original sin is derived by way of contrast to the prior concept of the new life of Christ made available in baptism, and is thus to be understood in contrast to the life of the Spirit lived in the communion of the Church. If St. Augustine led us to think of this contrast in terms of natural generation versus sacramental regeneration, a way of resolving the embarrassments provoked by some of the formulations deriving from this contrast (for example, on the inherent sinfulness of sexual activity even within a sacramental marriage) would be to highlight the mystery of the Church—and thus of the Christian family—as the embodied mystery of grace. Such an embodiment of God's eschatologically victorious grace in Jesus Christ is never totally unambiguous: we see now only as in a glass darkly. But the ambivalence of marriage and of the family is matched by the ambivalence of the Church itself as a social and historical institution, pointing beyond itself only more or less adequately, both being natural institutions as well as sacraments of life in Christ.

Just as the Church has consistently to remind herself and others of her otherworldly inner nature, so too must the family. This being so, the celebration of baptism for the forgiveness of sins, for the overcoming of alienation from God, would serve to reinforce the intentionality of the family in its specific role as a community of Christ's holiness and grace in the world. The dual nature of the Christian family requires a "double birth" for each new child: the one in the delivery room and the one in the baptistery.

Were the child of Christian parents not baptized, the opportunity of re-presenting its vocation to holiness would be passed up and the ambivalence of the family would be rendered all the more ambiguous. Correspondingly if a family merely "goes through the motions" of having its child baptized without at the same time taking stock of its own vocation to be a sacrament of grace and holiness, the child would be validly baptized as a member of the institutional Church, but the reality signified by membership of the Church—participation in the very life of God, which is forgiveness of sin—would be unlikely to be realized, and the shadow of original sin would still linger over the child precisely because that shadow would be cast by members of the family. The overcoming of original sin by the grace of Christ is not magic. It happens sacramentally, that is through signs. It happens because the rite is a sacrament of the faith of the Church which, where a small child is concerned, is in effect the faith of the family. Where the family does not consciously live the life of faith and grace, it is hard to see how baptism can then and there be fruitful for the forgiveness of sin. The child will have to await the effective intervention of some other representative of the faithful Church for its baptism to "revive" and to become fruitful in the life of grace and faith.[46]

The Child as Subject of Sacramental Initiation

For the historical reasons suggested above, children, especially the newborn, have traditionally been regarded as passive recipients of adult ministrations: clean tablets to be written on, clay to be molded by parental hands. Or else they were seen as active only in manifesting the signs of concupiscence, the fallen will. As Robert Pattison observes: "In the Augustinian view, the child is perhaps subrational, but this is of no importance and properly the business of philosophy, not religion. More important, the child is a creature of will, a sinner *ab ovo* and in this no different from adults."[47]

Such primitive psychotheologizing can no longer be entertained in the wake of the immense amount of research done in this century into the world of the child. Andrew Thompson's contribution to this volume will bring together an impressive array of insights into the child's experience of the world, especially in terms of the child's relationship to its parents and siblings. Rather than anticipate all aspects of Thompson's report and to avoid encroaching on Herbert Anderson's pastoral-theological territory, we shall be content here to highlight some aspects of this recovery of childhood which relate to the capacity of the child for sacramental initiation.

Before that can be done, however, there is a preliminary step to be taken. Unless there are good reasons for thinking that the child *as child* has some part in the economy of grace and may be called, precisely as a small child, to witness as part of the sacramentality of the whole Church which is "a sacrament or sign of intimate union with God and of the unity of all mankind" (LG, 1), there is a danger of romanticizing childhood and of reading into the life of the child salvific realities which are in fact suspended until such time as the child gradually acquires those adult characteristics of intellect, will, and which are the preconditions for their realization. But, as Karl Rahner has demonstrated, there is every reason to believe that childhood not only falls within the compass of God's grace, but that

> childhood itself has a direct relationship with God. It touches upon the absolute divinity of God not only as maturity, adulthood and the later phases of life touch upon this, but rather in a special way of its own . . . . The fact that it contributes to the later stages of life is not the sole criterion of its own intrinsic rightness.[48]

Not the least of our grounds for believing that this is the case is to be found in the Incarnation itself. "What was not assumed is not redeemed," is the old patristic axiom, but childhood was assumed. Irenaeus put this best:

> Christ came to save all [human beings] by himself: all, I say, who through him are reborn in God: infants and children, youths and adults, and the elderly. For this it was that he lived through every age [of life]: made an infant for the sake of infants; a child for the children, sanctifying those of that age and setting them an example of devotion, fairness and obedience; a youth for the sake of young people, becoming an example for them and sanctifying them for God . . . .[49]

Thus infants and young children are sanctified in principle insofar as the Son of God became a child and lived through childhood's experiences in total union with the will of the Father, thereby redeeming infancy and childhood. Thereafter, childhood lived in the Spirit of Christ—albeit necessarily in a preconscious and prereflective way—is sanctified and may be seen as a sign of the glory of God and of the unity of the redeemed human family.

Let us briefly spell out the implications of this with reference particularly to those aspects of the baptismal event which infant baptism might be supposed to obscure.

Faith and the Sacrament of Faith

While all the sacraments of the Church are sacraments of faith, the term applies particularly to baptism, which, from the New Testament onwards, has always included the candidate's profession of faith. It was for this reason that the Anabaptists and their successors have denied the validity of infant baptism, and that some modern Catholics have been led to question its value. There is no denying that the practice of having parents or godparents answer the faith interrogation on behalf of the child was inappropriate at best and a subterfuge at worst.[50] It was simply a way of getting around the fact that the candidate was *in statu infantis.* What helped compound the problem was the increasing tendency to consider faith primarily in cognitive terms.

It is not clear that St. Augustine had a conceptual understanding of faith in mind when he spoke of the child being baptized in the faith of the Church,[51] but this understanding was certainly operative in the twelfth and thirteenth centuries when the issue arose again.[52] Recognizing that a child cannot "believe" in the sense of making an active submission of the intellect, St. Thomas Aquinas taught that in baptism faith was infused as a habitus, which he defined as "a quality not easily removed, whereby one may act easily and pleasantly."[53] It is hard to see what sense can be made of the idea of "infusing" a child with the capacity for acts of faith, especially when the analogy is drawn, for the purposes of distinguishing between the virtue of faith and its exercise, between a child and a sleeping adult.

Instead of redefining faith to fit in with one's preconceived notions of infancy, however, it might be more fruitful to reconsider the child and its capacity for some kind of life of faith even in its status as an infant. Clearly an infant is prerational. If faith is conceived of simply as an act of grace-enlightened reason, then the child has nothing to do but wait until its rational capacities are sufficiently developed as to be able to cooperate with grace. Its Christian life, like its adult life, remains a thing of the future. But the Second Vatican Council moved to counter an excessively cognitive view of faith with a return to the Pauline concept of faith as an "obedience of faith," which it went on to define as that obedience "whereby a person entrusts his whole self freely to God."[54] Seen in this way, faith is primarily a way of being, marked by commitment to and dependence upon God. For an older child or an adult this will surely mean, as the council says, "offering full submission of intellect and will to God who reveals, and freely assenting to the truth revealed by him."[55] But this second part of the definition is a specification of what it means to entrust one's whole self freely to God, a specification which undoubtedly applies to all who have attained the use of reason, but which does not preclude the possibility that those such as infants and retarded adults might not also live a life of total dependence upon God. Indeed it is the infant and the "youngest child" who constantly bring the subversive message of the Gospel as salvation by obedience of faith to a Church constantly prone to place too much confidence in its intellectual respectability.[56]

James Fowler has proposed a view of faith which corresponds closely to the conciliar understanding of theological faith. In Fowler's view, faith need not be necessarily thought of as an exclusively religious phenomenon. "Rather," he suggests, "faith becomes the designation for a way of leaning into life. It points to a way of making sense of one's existence. It denotes a way of giving order and coherence to the force-field of life. It speaks of the investment of life-grounding trust and life-orienting commitment."[57]

As he goes on to point out, this understanding of faith "means to imply that it is a human universal." He traces its development through infancy and early childhood and argues that the development of faith of some kind, some sort of making sense of the world, some sense of what one may base one's trust on and what makes life worthwhile, is an inevitable development in every child. Even before it becomes articulate—if indeed it ever becomes articulate about its faith, for this "leaning into life" is rarely brought to full consciousness—the child comes to faith. The question then is less one of whether a child can "have" faith than it is a question of the kind of faith it comes in fact to exercise in the first weeks and months of life. There is no need to have recourse to St. Thomas Aquinas' distinction between *habitus* and *actus*, tailored as it is to a cognitive understanding of faith. With a precognitive understanding of faith, the child is seen, from the moment of its birth, to be enacting its developing faith as it encounters its human environment, experiences dependency and separation, shared meanings and ritual patterns, provision for its bodily needs, and a sense of its own social and sexual identity.[58] Faith is a holistic, prerational sense of who we are and of the kind of world we live in, an integrated vision of how things are and what it all means. From a theological perspective, then, what is at issue in the celebration of the sacraments is not so much whether the candidates have faith, but of whether their faith is faith in the God who raised Jesus from the dead. For adults this means that evangelizing is a matter of uprooting false faith as well as a matter of communicating true faith, a realization that has enormous implications for the catechumenate. For the children of the Church, it means forming them in right faith from infancy. To wait until they attain the use of reason is already to wait too long and to leave their faith to chance.

For Christians right faith is baptismal faith and baptismal faith is paschal faith. But how can infants be said to be baptized into such faith?

Paschal faith is the faith which was Christ's, the faith whereby he was made perfect through suffering and consistently surrendered his life into the hands of the God who alone could save him out of death (see Heb 5:7-8). Such a pattern, as something lived out by the community of the baptized, is what constitutes the faith of the Church. By baptism we have been fitted into a pattern of surrender and exaltation, of self-abandonment and deliverance, of dying and being raised. But such a pattern, far from being alien to the life of the child, is intrinsic to it. Having experienced the trauma of separation from the womb, the child is confronted with the task of learning to live as both autonomous and yet dependent, caught between the desire for communion and the need to accept separation, instinctively struggling to satisfy its own immediate needs yet learning to wait in trust for what it really needs. "The nerve to separate," says Fowler of the many experiences of separation and nonfulfillment in the infant's life, "depends upon the assured return to communion."[59]

Now this is clearly not the same as adult conversion (though it would seem to be something that would condition the very possibility of genuine adult conversion), but neither is it merely an illustration of some aspect of the paschal mystery. Is it not rather the paschal mystery as lived by every child that is born into this world? Or perhaps we should turn that around and say that Christ, in assuming our human condition, assumed the pattern which constitutes one of the most basic tasks of every human life and redeemed it. Unless we wish to withold the life of the small child altogether from the drama of redemption, must we not see here, *in statu infantis*, the primordial and universal pattern of human life which Christ assumed and redeemed? Is it not because of false faith, trust in false gods and false values, that sin has such an obvious hold upon the world? Sin cannot be reduced simply to individual, conscious, wilful acts. Similarly the redemptive gift of paschal faith, the Christlike way of "leaning into life," is not necessarily anything which has to await our conscious decision or deliberate choice. It is rather something which we discover to be already operative in us by the grace of God by the time we become aware of it.

This grace, this gift of faith, comes through hearing, through the Word of God addressed to the child. But the Word here is not the written Word, as yet unavailable to the infant, so much as the biblical *dabar*, the revelatory and salvific event of God's presence, mediated in this instance by the community of faith and especially the believing family. Thus it is not so much that baptism infuses faith into a child as that baptism is the deliberate and conscious insertion of the child into the environment of faith, which faith is the faith of the Church, which in turn is the faith of Christ himself. If the Church did not continue to live by the pattern of Christ's own faith in its dying and being raised to life, it would cease to be Church. Such existential faith constitutes the identity of the Church and the identity of the family as domestic church. It is into this faith that the child is baptized when it is baptized in the faith of the Church.

Integration into the Church

A major stumbling block to Anabaptist recognition of the validity of infant baptism is the view of the Church as a participative community of faith and mutual correction. Though situated at the opposite end of the baptismal spectrum, Roman Catholics seem to share the view that infants, being purely passive, are incapable of actively engaging in the life of the faith community. Believers' Churches apparently consider that the child has nothing to contribute to the faith life and witness of the local congregation, while Catholics, by neglecting small children between *quamprimum* baptism and the age of reason, seem to regard the child as unfit for active participation in community life. Why else should children, alone of all the baptized, be barred from confirmation and Eucharist?

In fact, however, as Andrew Thompson amply demonstrates, a newborn infant alters the configuration of family relationships from the day of its birth, if not sooner, having a major impact on the lives of its parents and siblings. Nor should this impact be seen as merely financial or psychological. The Second Vatican Council spoke perhaps more truly than it knew when it said: "As living members of the family, children contribute in their own way to making their parents holy" (GS, 48). Stanley Hauerwas puts the point more strongly when he writes that

> a good deal of sentimental drivel is written about children. Sentimentality not only belies the hard reality of caring for children, but worse, it avoids the challenge with which they confront us. Generally our children challenge the kind of self-image that finds its most intense expression in the expectations we have for them. If we are lucky, these expectations are modified by our children's refusal to be what we want them to be . . . . Children train us not only to be parents, but sometimes even better parents.[60]

Translating this into the terms of Christian theology, we might say that children bring both joy and the Cross. Children will test the sacrificial self-commitment, the self-delusions, and the spurious faith of those with whom they come in contact for any length of time. They summon parents particularly to a deeper understanding of the mystery of grace and of the limitations of human abilities. They probe the ambivalences of their "way of leaning into life." But they also evoke a spirit of wonder and benediction and become messengers of unsolicited consolation. All this is merely to suggest that in their own way children in fact play an extremely active, even prophetic, role in the household of faith. The obstacle lies not in the child but in the faithlessness of the adult believers. If there is any reason for not admitting an infant to faith and baptismal life in the communion of the Church, it may only be that the child's own God-given household is not faithful.

Theology of Baptism

We have already noted that one of the most significant effects of the introduction of the adult catechumenate and a unified rite of sacramental initiation for adults has been the recovery of a fuller and richer understanding of baptism. In comparison with the rich heritage of patristic teaching on baptism, most modern Christians have inherited a drastically impoverished understanding of the wealth and wonder of the baptismal life. As we also noted, there is sometimes a tendency to blame this impoverishment on infant baptism, though it would probably be more accurate to say that it is the result of the institutionalization of *emergency* baptism. Conversely, the recovery of the paschal dimensions of baptism is sometimes promoted in such a way as to challenge, if not to preclude altogether, the practice of infant initiation. We attempted to suggest that this conclusion need not necessarily follow, since while some aspects of a positive theology of baptism (for example, adoption) are very much congruent with the baptizing of small children, other aspects (for example, dying and rising) can be seen to be viable even for infants, provided the state of infancy is carefully considered. But besides the questions of faith and participation in the paschal mystery already touched on, there are other important dimensions of sacramental initiation which are actually highlighted by the baptism of a small child.

A newly baptized infant is not merely one who is delivered from sin and from the threat of damnation, but one claimed by the irrescindable Word of God to be an adopted child of God, a living member of Christ, a temple of the Holy Spirit. The child in baptism enters into a new set of relationships with God, with the Church, and—we have argued—with its own family. In this instance, at least, water is thicker than blood! From early in our tradition comes the story of the father of the great Alexandrian theologian, Origen. The historian Eusebius reports: "It is said that often when the boy was asleep, he would bend over him and bare his breast and, as if it were the temple of the Spirit of God, would kiss it reverently and count himself blessed in his promising child."[61]

St. John Chrysostom reflects the same sort of sentiment in an Easter sermon:

> Those who were prisoners yesterday are free men and citizens of the Church. Those who so recently were in sin and shame now enjoy righteousness and security. They are not only free, but holy; not only holy, but righteous; not only righteous, but children; not only children, but heirs; not only heirs, but brothers and sisters of Christ; not only brothers and sisters of Christ, but co-heirs with him; not only co-heirs with Christ, but members of him; not only members of Christ, but temples; not only temples, but instruments of the Holy Spirit.
> Blessed be God, for he has done wonders! (Ps 72:18) Do you realize how manifold are the blessings of baptism? While many believe that the remission of sins is the sole benefit of baptism, we have counted ten. That is why we baptize even tiny children, even though they have no sins, that they might gain righteousness, filiation, inheritance, and

the grace of being brother and sisters and members of Christ and the grace of being the dwelling-place of the Holy Spirit.[62]

Furthermore one must agree with Karl Barth that "too little attention has been paid to baptism as a glorifying of God, that is, as a moment of his self-revelation . . . . While baptism does its cognitive work . . . the far greater and primary thing occurs: God receives glory in that he himself, as man recognizes him in truth, once more secures his just due here on earth."[63]

Admittedly Barth is thinking here of believers' baptism, but his words apply equally well, it would seem, to infant baptism as an act of thanksgiving and glorification of God. But it is important to draw a clear distinction between infant baptism and various forms that exist for giving thanks for the birth of a child. While childbirth is itself a striking moment of religious disclosure—one sufficiently powerful to have lent itself and its terminology as a metaphor even for adult initiation—and while it is properly a moment for the blessing of God, baptism cannot be reduced to a celebration of birth. A service of thanksgiving for the safe delivery of a child should be an option for those whose faith extends so far, but who are uncertain as to the meaning of the order of redemption and of Christian baptism, and whose allegiance to the community of faith is consequently less than firm. But it should be clear to believers and unbelievers alike that baptism is more than a celebration of birth. It is, as we have already stressed, a celebration and sacrament of rebirth: it is incorporation into the Body of Christ and into the pattern of his death and exaltation; it is a divine act of adoption, whereby a child is claimed by God for his own kind purposes; it is a consecration and sanctification effected by the outpouring of the Holy Spirit of Christ; it is an anointing with the Spirit of holiness for life and mission in this world and for the sanctification of the divine Name, in this world and in the world to come.

All this belongs to a child in principle, as surely and as undeservedly as the kingdom belongs to the heir apparent. Like many an heir apparent, the Christian child may be defrauded of its birthright, may even grow up knowing nothing of it. But, for all that, baptism remains a performative act with certain ineluctable entailments which, even though they be frustrated by the faithlessness of the family or parish, remain nevertheless eternally valid.

Since the practice of infant baptism predates the Augustinian doctrine of original sin, and since that doctrine has not played the major role in the East that it has in the West, one must assume that it is these positive benefits of baptism which have long underlain the Church's instinct to admit infants and small children to the font and the altar. In any case the practice of baptizing infants does not depend for its legitimacy upon the belief that without baptism infants are excluded forever from the vision of God. But it does suppose the possibility that infants *as infants* might be called to share the divine life in the Body of Christ, a possibility which, as we have argued, derives substantial support both from the fact that the Church has always baptized infants and from the insights into the nature of childhood gained from the research of the human sciences.

But while every human being is called to share the life of God, it is obvious that not every human being is called to live as a member of the Church. In the case of an infant born into a believing family, however, there is an a priori assumption that the fact of its being born into an ecclesial community constitutes a reasonable indication that this child is called by God to grace and to glory within the communion of the visible Church. This has nothing to do with John Calvin's assertion that the Old Testament precept concerning circumcision continues to operate under the new covenant. On the contrary, the distinctions we have made between first birth and second birth, between baptism and a celebration of thanksgiving, clearly indicate that Christian identity is precisely *not* inherited from Christian parents, but that the "accident" of being born into a practicing Christian household is rather an indication of the child's vocation, which it is the duty of the Church to affirm, ratify, and nurture. Consequently whenever a child is presented for baptism, it will be the responsibility of the local community to discern whether this child is certainly called to the life of faith by looking at the faith life of the family. More positively, those with pastoral responsibilities will take seriously the ecclesial character of the family as a household of faith and seek to raise the community's awareness of the sacramentality of the family.

Infant Baptism as a Sacrament for the Church

There was a time when the definition of a sacrament tended to focus on the matter and form of each sacrament, thus tending to depersonalize the sacraments. The twentieth-century renewal of sacramental theology has overcome this narrow and static understanding by seeing the sacraments more dynamically as an interaction between the recipient and the minister who, representing the Church, represents Christ. More recently the public and ecclesial dimension of the sacraments has been recovered, enabling us to recognize that sacraments, when properly celebrated, are meant to redound to the benefit not only of the recipient but of the whole ecclesial community. Such an understanding finds authoritative expression, for example, in the General Introduction to the Order of Penance which goes so far as to say that "the faithful Christian, as he experiences and proclaims the mercy of God in his life, celebrates with the priest *the liturgy with which the Church continually renews itself"* (par. 11, emphasis added).

The truth of this axiom is, of course, even more apparent in the experience of the RCIA, which is teaching us that the initiation of new members not only affects their own lives, but calls for new configurations of relationships within the host community itself.

In infant baptism, we have argued, the ecclesial ramifications of the rite have immediate importance for the family, which is reconstituted by the liturgy of baptism in its God-given identity as a household of faith, a domestic church. Thus the importance of the renewal of baptismal promises (for the parents no longer speak in the name of the child, but in their own name) consists in the fact that the making of the promises is a sacramental act as well as a moral commitment: it is the family actualizing itself as a domestic household of faith within the communion of the local assembly. The formulae of renunciation and profession of faith are, as it were, words of consecration whereby the local Church confects itself as a living sacrament of faith. This perspective on the family-as-ecclesial-sacrament enables us then to grasp more profoundly what is meant by speaking of the parents in particular as the child's "first teachers of the faith." Stanley Hauerwas makes this point more broadly applicable when he says that the Church does not *do* religious education, but *is* a form of education that is religious.

> Religious education is not . . . something that is done to make us Christians, or something that is done after we have become Christians; rather it is the ongoing training in those skills necessary for us to live faithful to God's Kingdom that has been initiated in Jesus. For that Kingdom is constituted by a story that one never possesses, but rather constantly challenges us to be what we have not yet become.[64]

Consequently, parents do not so much promise at their children's baptism to teach them merely what they know. Instead, they commit themselves anew to learning the story by living it, and it is chiefly by the parents living the Christian story that their children will come to pick it up and to develop the skills necessary to be faithful to it. The story and the skills are only partially conveyed in explicit lessons. Christianity, it has been said, is more caught than taught, and the model for learning it is closer to that of an apprenticeship than that of a classroom. In this apprenticeship the accent is on doing the things that Christians do, which makes the practice of withholding from small children the anointing of the Spirit and regular participation at the Eucharistic table all the more unfortunate.[65] It suggests that these sacraments are rewards for lessons learned or markers in the child's growth to maturity, instead of being what they are, namely, the means of our continuing formation in Christian fidelity.

But besides the immediate liturgical sacramental dimensions of infant baptism for the family and the local church, there is also the question of whether, when the sacraments of initiation are made accessible to small children, something important is not gained for the Church's own self-understanding. This is not the place to discuss whether and in what sense adult initiation might be said to be "normative," but even if this were to be admitted, it could not be used to disparage the practice of infant initiation as such, except at the cost of departing from the Catholic tradition or at least sacrificing significant elements of that tradition. N. P. Williams in *The Ideas of the Fall and Original Sin*[66] identifies two sets of conflicting ideas in the theology of redemption: those associated with what he calls the image of the "once born" and those associated with the image of being "twice born." The former gives rise to a theology which stresses continuity and growth in human life, the latter to a theology which highlights conversion and discontinuity. While we would resist, for reasons given earlier, any attempt to describe infants who are baptized as "once born," the contrast between a theology of continuity and a theology of discontinuity accurately summarizes the differences between those who support infant baptism and those who see it as difficult to reconcile with the evangelical values manifest in adult conversion and adult initiation.

Adult baptism, the economy of the "twice born," tends to draw to itself the vocabulary of regeneration as opposed to generation; of brothers and sisters rather than sons and daughters; of voluntary decision rather than divine vocation; of change rather than faithfulness; of breaking with the past rather than growth towards the future; of death and resurrection rather than adoption and filiation. The language of infant initiation, on the other hand, is inclined to speak in terms of the womb rather than the tomb, of election rather than choice, of loyalty rather than commitment, of the preconscious operations of grace rather than of personal convictions, of nurturing the life of faith rather than of passing from unbelief to belief. In Jungian terms, a regime which attaches importance to infant initiation gives a larger role to the "feminine" aspects of Christianity, while adult initiation displays the more "masculine" elements of Christian imagery.

While there are many other and stronger reasons for upholding the baptism of infants, this would seem a further argument for retaining it. At a time when the Church is so intent on rescuing the humane values of Christianity and is concerned to do greater justice to the role of the family and to the Christian vision of sexuality, and at a time when the role of the nonrational and prerational dimensions of the life of faith is being recovered,[67] perhaps infant initiation ought to be seen less as a problem to be grappled with than as an opportunity to be grasped. Far from barring children from the font, the chrism, and the altar, the Church should welcome their participation in these sacraments as a reminder both of the catholicity of the Church and of the fact that, no matter how informed or committed we might be as adults, when we take part in the sacramental liturgies of the Church we are taking part in more than we know.

Conclusion

Historically speaking, the practice of infant baptism always seems to have preceded and in some ways eluded attempts to justify it theologically. It seems to have been more a matter of the Church's instinct than the putting into effect of a clearly thought-out strategy, while attempts to make sense of it have always fallen short of success. Similarly with this chapter. It would be foolish to claim that the argument is now settled, but it may legitimately be claimed, if the arguments advanced here hold water, that the grounds of the discussion need to be changed. This in turn will influence practice, since a fresh grasp of what is involved in baptizing an infant will suggest ways of assessing when baptism may properly be celebrated for infants, how it may be prepared for, and most importantly how it may be lived in a process of ongoing initiation to the life of faith in the context of family and parish. Central to this reconsideration of baptism, however, will be theological reflection on the data of the human sciences concerning the child-in-relationship. It is precisely such data that the next chapter will present.

Footnotes

1. Stephen W. Sykes, "The Sacraments," in *Christian Theology*, eds. Peter C. Hodgson and Robert H. King, rev. ed. (Philadelphia: Fortress, 1985) 274–301.

2. Among a very extensive literature, the following must be accounted the most significant works: Oscar Cullmann, *Baptism in the New Testament* (London: S.C.M., 1950); Karl Barth, *The Teaching of the Church Concerning Baptism* (London: S.C.M., 1948); Karl Barth, *Church Dogmatics*, IV:4 (Edinburgh: T. & T. Clark, 1969); Markus Barth, *Die Taufe ein Sakrament?* (Zollikon-Zurich, 1951); Kurt Aland, *Did the Early Church Baptize Infants?* (Philadelphia: Westminster Press, 1960); Joachim Jeremias, *Infant Baptism in the First Four Centuries* (Philadelphia: Westminster Press, 1960). More recently see Paul Jewett, *Infant Baptism and the Covenant of Grace* (Grand Rapids: Eerdmans, 1978) and Geoffrey W. Bromiley, *Children of Promise* (Grand Rapids: Eerdmans, 1979).

3. J. D. C. Fisher, *Christian Initiation. Baptism in the Medieval West. A Study in the Disintegration of the Primitive Rite of Initiation*, Alcuin Club, n. 47 (London: S.P.C.K., 1965). See *Catechism of the Council of Trent*, II, iii, 17 (Dublin: J. Duffy and Co., 1829) 183.

4. Eusebius, *The History of the Church*, VI, 43:20, trans. G.A. Williamson (Minneapolis: Augsburg, 1975) 283.

5. E. C. Whitaker, *Documents of the Baptismal Liturgy*, Alcuin Club, n. 42 (London: S.P.C.K., 1970) 222–223.

6. Cfr. M. Righetti, *Storia liturgica*, IV (Milan, 1953) 82–83; P. de Puniet, *Le sacramentaire romain de Gellone*. Bibliotheca Ephemerides Liturgicae, IV, Rome, 1938, 90–91.

7. DS 1349.

8. P.-M. Gy, *"Quamprimum*. Note sur le baptême des enfants," *La Maison Dieu* 32 (1952) 124–129.

9. See note 3 above.

10. Interest in the history of childhood is relatively recent, largely inaugurated by Philippe Ariès' benchmark study, *Centuries of Childhood* (New York: Knopf, 1962). For a reassessment of Ariès' claims, see *The History of Childhood*, Lloyd de Mausse, ed. (New York: The Psychohistory Press, 1974) and David Hunt, *Parents and Children in History. The Psychology of Family Life in Early Modern France* (New York: Basic Books, 1970). It is now clear that the "age of reason" or "age of discretion," typically identified in Roman Catholic sources as around the age of seven to ten years, is less a determinate stage of psychological maturity than a juridical-social convention. Thus under Anglo-Saxon law a child who reached the age of seven could no longer be sold into slavery, while under Roman Law a child of that age became liable for criminal acts. In general it was the age at about which children began to mix with adults in medieval life and work.

11. So Cullmann, *Baptism in the New Testament* 72–78 and Joachim Jeremias, *Infant Baptism* 48–55. For an opposing viewpoint see G. R. Beasley-Murray, *Baptism in the New Testament* (Grand Rapids: Eerdmans, 1973) 320–329.

12. Kurt Aland, *Did the Early Church Baptize Infants?*

13. *de baptismo*, 18. (ET: *Tertullian's Homily on Baptism*, trans. E. Evans [London: S.P.C.K., 1964] 36–38.)

14. *de anima* 39–40, C.S.L., II, 842–843.

15. D. Michaélides, *Sacramentum chez Tertullien* (Paris: Etudes augustiniennes, 1970).

16. *de baptismo*, 19.

17. The most celebrated instance of the deferment of baptism is St. Augustine himself. See *The Confessions of St. Augustine*, Bk. I, ch. 11, trans. John K. Ryan (Garden City, N.Y.: Image Books, 1960) 53–54.

18. See Margaret Miles, "Infancy, Parenting and Nourishment in St. Augustine's Confessions," *Journal of the American Academy of Religion* 50 (1982) 3, 349–364.

19. *Ibid.* 355.

20. St. Augustine, *The City of God*, XXI, 4.

21. *De ecclesiasticarum rerum exordiis et incrementis*, c. 27, text in J.-Ch. Didier, *Faut-il baptiser les enfants? La réponse de la tradition* (Paris: Cerf), 239–240.

22. *Sentences*, V:6, text in Didier, *Faut-il baptiser les enfants?* 256.

23. *Summa Theologiae*, Pars III, q. 69, art. 6.

24. See Louis Dumont, "A Modified View of Our Origins: The Christian Beginnings of Modern Individualism," *Religion* 12 (1982) 1–27.

25. H. Schwartz, "Early Anabaptist Ideas about the Nature of Children," *The Mennonite Quarterly Review* 47 (1973) 2, 104. See also James McClendon, "Why Baptists Do Not Baptize Children," *Concilium* 24 (1967) 7–14.

26. For a summary of Luther's and Calvin's views on infant baptism, see E. Schlink, *The Doctrine of Baptism*, trans. H. J. A. Bouman (St. Louis: Concordia, 1972) 130–170.

27. For the main literature see note 2 above.

28. Henri Bourgeois, "The Catechumenate in France Today," in *Becoming a Catholic Christian*, ed. W. J. Reedy (New York: Sadlier, 1979) 10–21.

29. *Ordo initiationis christianae adultorum*, 1972 (ET: 1974, 1985).

30. Aidan Kavanagh, *The Shape of Baptism* (New York: Pueblo, 1978) 109–114, 196–197. For an overview of Roman Catholic discussions of infant baptism, see Paul F. X. Covino, "The Postconciliar Infant Baptism Debate in the American Catholic Church," *Worship* 56 (1982) 240–260.

31. Avery Dulles, *Models of the Church* (New York: Doubleday, 1974).

32. R.-M. Roberge, "Un tournant dans la pastorale du baptême," *Laval Theologique et Philosophique* 31 (1975) 227–238 and 33 (1977) 3–22.

33. *Rite for the Christian Initiation of Adults* (Washington: I.C.E.L. 1985) n. 41. See also Congregation for the Doctrine of the Faith, *Instruction on Infant Baptism* (Oct. 20, 1980) nn. 30–31. English text in *Origins* 10:30 (January 8, 1981) 479.

34. Kavanagh, *The Shape of Baptism*, 199. For a trenchant review of Kavanagh's position, see T. A. Droege, "The Formation of Faith in Christian Initiation," *The Cresset* 66 (1983) 6, 16–23.

35. Antonius Scheer, "Is the Easter Vigil a Rite of Passage?" in *Liturgy and Human Passage*, eds. David N. Power and Luis Maldonado (Concilium, 112) (New York: Seabury, 1979) 50–61.

36. André Benoit, *Le baptême chretien au 2e siècle* (Paris: Presses Universitaires de France, 19).

37. On the Syrian baptismal tradition see S. Brock, "Studies in the Early History of the Syrian Orthodox Baptismal Liturgy," *Journal of Theological Studies*

n.s. 23 (1972) 16–64; Gabriele Winkler, "The Original Meaning of the Prebaptismal Anointing and Its Implications," *Worship* 42 (1978) 24–45; S. J. Beggiani, *Early Syriac Theology* (Lanham, Md.: University Press of America, 1983) 101–124.

38. Robert Pattison, *The Child Figure in English Literature* (Athens, Ga.: The University of Georgia Press, 1978) 5–6.

39. David Hunt, *Parents and Children in History*, 190.

40. Nineteenth-century changes in cultural attitudes towards children and in corresponding approaches to childrearing appear to have been reflected in a gradual abandonment of the classical Augustinian teaching on original sin. See Bernard Wishy, *The Child and the Republic. The Dawn of Modern American Child Nurture* (Philadelphia: University of Pennsylvania Press, 1968); H. Sheldon Smith, *Changing Conceptions of Original Sin. A Study in American Theology since 1750* (New York: Scribners, 1955).

41. Karl Rahner, "Ideas for a Theology of Childhood," *Theological Investigations*, vol. VIII (New York: Herder & Herder, 1971) 33–50; Randolph C. Miller, "Theology and the Understanding of Children," *The Nature of Man in Theological and Psychological Perspective* ed. Simon Doniger (New York: Harper & Row, 1962) 142–150; Nathan Mitchell, "The Parable of Childhood," *Liturgy* 1 (1981) 3, 7–12; Guy Bédouelle, "Reflections on the Place of the Child in the Church," *Communio* 12 (1985) 4, 349–367.

42. See P. M. Zulehner, "Religionssoziologie und Kindertaufe" in *Christsein Ohne Entscheidung, oder Soll die Kirche Kinder Taufen?* ed., Walter Kasper (Mainz: Grünewald, 1970) 188–206.

43. See *Rite for the Baptism of Children*, n. 70. See also nn. 5, 39, 56, 64.

44. Second Vatican Council *Dogmatic Constitution on the Church*, n. 11; *Pastoral Constitution on the Church in the Modern World*, n. 48; *Decree on the Apostolate of the Laity*, n. 11; *Decree on Christian Education*, n. 3. The reference to the sacrament of marriage is not intended to preclude the possibility that single parent families or irregular marriages might not de facto be microchurches in virtue of the quality of the faith life and public witness of such families, but merely to underline the sacramental and ecclesial dimension formally established by a marriage witnessed by the Church.

45. The willingness of the Church in the past to baptize dying infants without even consulting the parents is simply one aspect of the diminished sign value of emergency baptism. Other aspects would include the absence of an ecclesial community, the celebration of baptism outside the Easter season, the lack of a full ritual setting, and the omission of confirmation and Eucharist. Unfortunately scholastic theology of the sacraments took such extreme cases as the starting point for a theology of baptism. The Second Vatican Council repudiated this approach by making the fullness of the sacramental sign, in all its communitarian and ritual dimensions, normative. See *Constitution on the Liturgy*, nn. 26, 27, 67.

46. This view is consistent with that of Augustine (Ep. 98, 10) that the child unlike the adult cannot place an obstacle to the grace of the sacraments. Recognizing the mediation of the family in the sacramental process also necessitates recognizing that the family itself may constitute an obstacle to the child's life of grace.

47. Pattison, *The Child Figure*, 18.

48. Rahner, "Ideas for a Theology of Childhood" 36–37.

49. *Adversus haereses*, II, 22.4. Text in Didier, *Faut-il baptiser les enfants?* 95.

50. It is to be noted that in the Roman Catholic *Rite for the Baptism of Children*, the parents and godparents profess their own faith and do not presume to speak for the child. See nn. 2 (Latin text) and 56.

51. St. Augustine uses *fides* and *credere* in several different if related ways. On the meaning of faith for Augustine, see among others: J. M. Egan, " 'I believe in God': I. The Doctrine of St. Augustine," *Irish Ecclesiastical Record* 53 (1939), 630–636; R. Aubert, *Le probleme de l'acte de la foi* (Louvain: Warny, 1945) 21–30; M. Loehrer, *Der Glaubensbegriff des hl. Augustinus* (Einsiedeln: Benziger Verlag, 1955); Chr. Mohrmann, "Credere deo, credere deum, credere in deum," in *Melanges J. de Ghellink*. Gembloux: Eds. J. Duculot, 1951, vol. I, 277–285.

52. See note 10 above.

53. *Summa Theologiae*, Pars III, q. 69, art. 4. See also III, q. 68, art. 9 and q. 69, art. 3. On the meaning of "faith" for St. Thomas, see Wilfrid Cantwell Smith, *Faith and Belief* (Princeton: Princeton University Press, 1979) 78–91. See also *Ibid.* 70–78 on faith/*credo* in relation to baptism.

54. *Dogmatic Constitution on Divine Revelation*, n. 5.

55. *Ibid.*

56. See R. Haughton, *Tales from Eternity* (New York: Seabury, 1973) 19–49.

57. James Fowler, "Perspectives on the Family from the Standpoint of Faith Development Theory," *Perkins Journal*, Fall 1979, 7.

58. Erik Erikson. *Toys and Reasons. Stages in the Ritualization of Experience* (New York: Norton, 1977) esp. 85–92.

59. Fowler, "Perspectives on the Family" 3.

60. Stanley Hauerwas, "Learning Morality from Handicapped Children," *The Hastings Center Report*, October 1980, 45.

61. Eusebius, *History of the Church*, VI, 2:15. *Ed. cit.*, 241.

62. St. John Chrysostom, *Baptismal Homily III*, 5–6, text in Didier, *Faut-il baptiser les enfants?* 111–112.

63. Karl Barth, *The Teaching of the Church Concerning Baptism*, 31.

64. Stanley Hauerwas, "The Gesture of a Truthful Story: The Church and Religious Education," *Encounter* 43 (1982) 319–329.

65. While the Churches have begun to give more consideration to the presence of pre-school children at the liturgy (see, for example, R.C.D. Jasper [ed.] *Worship and the Child*. Essays by the Joint Liturgical Group [London: S.P.C.K., 1975]), serious attention to the issue of infant Communion is mainly confined to the Anglican churches. See, *Communion Before Confirmation?* Church Information Office (London, 1985) and *Nurturing Children in Communion*, Grove Liturgical Studies, n. 44 (Bramcote, Notts., 1985). See also, David Holeton, *Infant Communion Then and Now*. Grove Liturgical Studies, n. 27 (Bramcote, Notts., 1981).

66. N. P. Williams, *The Ideas of the Fall and Original Sin* (London and New York: Longmans, Green, 1927).

67. Vatican II retains the definition of faith given at Vatican I ("the full submission of intellect and will to God who reveals") but subordinates it to the broader concept of an "obedience of faith," thus making submission of intellect and will the form that such obedience will take for those already endowed with intellect and will, but leaving open the possibility that those not so endowed—infants, young children, and the retarded—might still be said to be capable of faith. In any case, intellective and voluntary capacities vary enormously from person to person and of themselves do not adequately describe the full scope of personal life that is being claimed by the grace of God.

2. INFANT BAPTISM IN THE LIGHT OF THE HUMAN SCIENCES

Andrew D. Thompson

Introduction

The contribution made by this chapter rests upon two premises which we would do well to identify from the outset. The first premise is that the process of religious initiation can be legitimately and usefully understood as an instance of socialization into a culture. The second premise is that all initiation—including Christian initiation, whether of infants or adults—is marked by paradox or dialectic, which are absolutely essential to development and growth, whether it be the growth of the individual or of the community. These two premises need some further elaboration and justification, but let us first identify what we mean by initiation.

Societies flourish and cultures survive because each generation hands on to the next the cumulative wisdom it has in its possession. In fact it is precisely a certain continuity-amid-discontinuity in patterns of living, working, relating, celebrating, and dying which gives a culture its identity and style. It is this dynamic tradition that allows us to recognize a multitude of individuals as constituting a particular society. The process of handing on the values, styles, outlooks, and lore of a society—its culture—is what we shall be referring to when we use the term initiation in this chapter. The content of initiation, what is handed on, is, of course, very complex. It may well include the imparting of instruction in such practical skills as hunting, gardening, cooking, housing, or the art of living in community. It may well include instruction in religious beliefs, the teaching of language skills, introduction to the economic system, and many other forms of know-how. But the important idea to grasp is that, whatever bits of knowledge or kinds of skill are being imparted, initiation is much more than the simple sharing of factual information. Initiation is the introduction of newcomers to a whole way of life in a community, including how its members relate to one another.

When initiation is spoken of, as here, in terms of handing on knowledge or introducing a person to a community and to its world view, we need to be careful that we do not assume that ready-made values are simply "deposited" in the initiate. Certainly in the course of the process, the initiate comes to adopt the point of view of the instructing community. But this is not a one-sided affair. Rather, the individual needs to be seen as assimilating, reworking, and appropriating the community's tradition, while the community itself has to adjust to the newcomer in its midst and, to a greater or lesser degree, allow itself to be influenced by the arrival of the newcomer.

So far we have spoken of initiation as a broad cultural process which most of the time is going on everywhere. In the absence of any compelling evidence to the contrary, it seems appropriate to assume that initiation into a religious culture or community will share most of the same characteristic features as these other forms of socialization. In other words by studying what happens when people are initiated into different cultures, we can identify some of the dynamics or principles which are operative when people become members of a religious culture. Such an assumption is consistent with the perspectives of cultural anthropology which affirm that religion broadly understood is itself a culture or a world view which depicts what its adherents believe to be "really real."[1] If a religion can legitimately be regarded as a cultural system, then the sharing of that culture in religious initiation is a form of cultural socialization. To say this is not to reduce religious initiation to a form of social determinism, nor to deny the transcendental aspects of the sacramental experience. It is merely to offer a new perspective in which to explore the depths of the mystery of Christian initiation.

It is already clear from the adoption of this rather broad perspective on initiation that the actual process of initiation must be both tensive and complex.

TENSIVE

Since initiation consists, as we have seen, in a value-sharing interaction between a community and an individual or group of individuals, there will always be some question or tension concerning how far the individual will go in accepting what the community wants to pass on. If, for example, the individual completely and wholeheartedly adopts the values of the community, it may be at the expense of sacrificing his or her own individuality. If, on the other hand, the individual were to reject the values proposed by the community, he or she would never be at home in that community and may become isolated and rootless. If individuality is stressed to the exclusion of community values, isolation may be the result; if the community swallows up the individual, conformism will triumph over individuality.

There are many such conflicting or paradoxical elements involved in the process of initiation, and we shall examine them in some depth shortly. Here we have suggested a tension between individuality and conformity to be characteristic of the initiation process. Such tension is not necessarily bad. Indeed it is potentially a very positive dynamic in human life, the constant struggle for healthy equilibrium. Erik Erikson's insistence that all psychosocial development hinges upon keeping such tensions alive throughout one's lifespan is well known,[2] as is Jean Piaget's description of intelligence (in the sense of know-how) as the maintaining of a proper balance between the individual and the environment.[3]

COMPLEX

Initiation is a process which is also characterized by complexity. The human spirit is mysterious and complicated, and the forces that nourish it are many. Such is the conclusion not only of poets but of empirical researchers, who have probed the psychological and environmental factors which might be thought to shape the growth of individuals and communities. Respect for the complexity of the forces at play in the interaction of person and environment is generally recognized by research today as the proper context within which to try to understand empirical findings. Such at least is the perspective of this writer, who is not at all convinced that the use of empirical research into socialization will inevitably lead to a deterministic view of initiation or to mechanistic methods of intervention. Nor does it supply pastoral ministers with direct answers to their quandaries; still less does it equip them to manipulate their parishioners by adjusting the ritual controls. For fifty years Jean Piaget undertook research into the psychology of child development, but he studiously avoided making suggestions about how educators or parents could or should promote the child's development. Like Piaget many researchers today are well aware that each individual's life is made up of innumerable factors, any of which could affect the individual's personal development. Even if the model of physical causality were valid in human affairs, elements of a person's history, his or her social network, economic involvement, and religious beliefs and practices interact in such complex ways that it would be impossible to isolate any single causes for human and religious development with any kind of scientific accuracy. So it is important to be quite clear about the nature of this exercise: we are specifically concerned with identifying some of the forces at work in the process of development and socialization we call initiation. Identifying complexity as one of the chief characteristics of the initiatory process is a way of acknowledging that while the findings we offer here will—it is hoped—shed some light on the process of initiation, they will not allow us to set up an initiation process whose outcome would be reliably predictable.

For the purposes of this chapter a number of studies have been consulted whose findings seem in the author's judgement to shed light on socialization processes which are also operative in Christian initiation, as this is undertaken for children born of believing Christian parents. Since even this literature is very extensive, it is surveyed here under the headings of seven principles which serve to summarize the findings—or at least the directions—indicated in the literature. It would be tempting, however, to try to apply these seven principles to pastoral practice just as they are unless the two characteristics of initiation, complexity and tensiveness, are borne in mind. The principles themselves are almost all constructed upon the acknowledgement of a certain dialectic or paradox or conflict of opposites at work in the initiation process. For these reasons it seems important that we first devote some further consideration to the phenomenon of the dialectic before moving on to a consideration of the principles themselves.

Part One: The Dialectics of Development

DIALECTIC: ITS ROLE IN PERSONALITY DEVELOPMENT

In almost any area of life one cares to consider, it is more or less clear that the processes at work in that area of life consist of continuing tension between opposing or complementary forces. In the world studied by physics, for example, the positive and negative poles which create an electrical charge or the magnetic attraction exerted by north and south poles are easily recognized instances of such forces. In human affairs we have the energy created in the field of economics by the forces of supply and demand, while in the area of human thought there is the famous dialectic of thesis and antithesis proposed by Hegelian philosophy. These are all examples of dialectic, which for the purposes of this study can be defined as dynamic tension between opposing and relatively equal forces.

The kind of dialectic we have in mind here, however, is the different kinds of tensions involved in the development of the individual in the context of community. Everyone experiences the tensions and sometimes the problems created by the conflicting demands of individual needs and social claims and responsibilities. Because each of them approaches the mystery of the human person from a different starting point and investigates it from a different angle, various classic schools of psychology have identified the dialectical processes in individual and social life in different ways, as the following table shows:

Author	School	Identification of Dialectic
Jean Piaget	cognitive developmentalists	equilibration of assimilation/accommodation
Lawrence Kohlberg	moral developmentalists	dissonance between stages
Erik Erikson	Neo-Freudian	balancing affective tensions
Carl Jung	psychoanalytic	balancing conscious/unconscious
Wilson Key	psychology of advertising	balancing subliminal/conscious
Victor Turner	social anthropology	conflict of structure/antistructure

Each of these psychological schools, together with Victor Turner's work on social order in anthropology, concur in pointing to the presence of dialectic both in individual growth and in the social order. Thus there appears to be a series of inevitable and necessary conflicts operative *within* the individual person, *between* individuals, and *between* the individual and the society of which he or she is a part. In other words most of the important and influential studies of the individual and of the individual in relation to society find some sort of dialectic—though they do not necessarily use that term—to be central to human development. We are bundles of contradictions and creatures of paradox, but it seems that without the contradictions and the paradoxes there would be no life and no growth.

Each of the theorists named uses some kind of dialectical model of human functioning and proposes it as a symbol system, which psychologists and clients may use to interpret experience, untangle relationships, and enhance appropriate behavior. Since, as we have already mentioned, the idea of dialectical processes is going to be a very important thread running through our seven principles, it might be helpful to suggest a little more of the richness of this concept by commenting briefly on how some of the above-named clinicians have expounded the theme in their own work.

Developmental Psychology

Three leading theorists in the field of psychological development are Jean Piaget (development of intelligence), Lawrence Kohlberg (moral development), and James Youniss (development of a social identity).

The work of Jean Piaget in studying how intelligence develops and blossoms in the child has demonstrated that intelligence is ultimately a matter of the child's being able to coordinate appropriate means to achieving given ends.[4] In order to do this, the person has to be able to deal with the flow of information coming in from the world around. Some of this information can be dealt with in terms of the person's existing frames of reference (assimilation), but sometimes the new information will require him or her to change their way of thinking in order to make room for it (accommodation). A person's ability to cope effectively with the world, then, depends upon what Piaget calls equilibration, a balance between the self and the environment. If the mind is too open, it will lose its bearings; if it is too rigid or too closed, it will be unable to handle new information.

An illustration of this principle is provided by Piaget in his description of the dialectic between play and imitation. What Piaget calls play occurs when the child imposes his or her ideas or images upon reality without attending to what that reality is actually like. There is an overreliance on assimilation, reality has to correspond to the child's preconceptions or illusions. On the other hand, when the child is so oriented to external realities that it is dominated by them, it is allowing those external realities to override the child's ability to cope with them on the child's own terms. This Piaget calls imitation.

What is significant about Piagetian epistemology and its description of intelligence, is that it demonstrates that meaning is neither something invented by a person, nor something simply given to that person, but rather the result of an interaction between self and world. Meaning is the result of a dialectic between inner self and outer world, while intelligence is the ability to keep that healthy dialectic going. Growth in maturity, socialization, and adaptation to one's inherited culture all depend upon the individual's being able to share meaning with his or her community. The dialectics we have mentioned between means and ends, between assimilation and accommodation, between playing and imitating, are simply examples of how the individual has continually to find a balance between the reality of the self and the reality of the community. Only through such a dialectic can the individual in fact enter into community through the sharing of common meanings.

A second generation of developmental psychologists include Lawrence Kohlberg who, in his work at Harvard, has elaborated an extensive framework for describing growth in moral understanding.[5] His six stages of moral development are well known, especially to educators. But what is less commonly recognized is the way Kohlberg presents an individual's understanding of moral justice as being driven forward by the experience of dissonance.

Dissonance is yet another form of dialectic. For Kohlberg this refers primarily to the contrast between the relatively simple structures of one stage of moral development and the relatively more complex structures of the next stage. This is "inter-stage dissonance." However, there are also forms of dissonance or discrepancy to be found even within the same stage, a form of dialectic which promises to be even more interesting.[6]

Kohlberg's work has made us aware of something that has enormous implications for pastoral work, not least in the area of pastoral care of families. His studies have shown that too much dissonance between stages—as when a preacher advocates a kind of morality too developed for most of his congregation, or a priest counsels love to those still bound in a morality of law—leads to a situation where those at the earlier level will simply fail to understand what is being said, and the opportunity for moral growth will be lost. Or to take an example nearer to the topic of this book, relatively sophisticated explanations of baptism in terms of death and resurrection or illumination are probably too abstract for most parishioners to be able to understand. This does not mean that most Catholics are too naive to be able to understand the mysteries we celebrate. Rather, it suggests we do well to follow the example of the Scriptures and the liturgy, using symbolic language and imagery which allow people to relate to the event at more than one level. In that way everyone present can get something out of the event and may be drawn beyond their previous level of moral and intellectual growth.

Yet a third generation of developmental psychologists is represented by James Youniss, who has researched the social development of children and the social dimensions of their intellectual and moral development.[7] Youniss looks at childhood development in terms of its environmental influences and the effect of the child's relationships with other people. Here too a dialectic is at work in very important ways. Youniss's research seems to show that moral development is particularly affected by peer relationships, especially after the child reaches the age of about ten. Peer relations foster moral development, while moral development is likely to be hindered if the child only has unilateral relationships, that is, those with authority figures. This dialectic then can be described as mutual versus unilateral. What it means is that a child is likely to mature more quickly in its moral judgements if it has lots of opportunities to mix with its peers and negotiate decisions in an atmosphere of friendship. Such developmental experience will be sorely missed if the child is kept away from other children and solely made to obey its parents. This is because, among children of the same age group, decisions are more likely to be arrived at in an open, democratic manner, rather than imposed by parental dictate. On the other hand, a child cannot live without some parental or other authority in its life. Hence comes the dialectic: the need for authority figures the child can trust and respect and the contrasting need for friends with whom the child can negotiate.

Neo-Freudian Psychology

It is nearly a century now since Sigmund Freud began to publish his clinical evidence to show that many people were living their lives more under the influence of unconscious than of conscious factors. Empirical research has only served to confirm this part of Freud's theory, and it has demonstrated furthermore that unconscious or irrational behavior is not restricted by any means to those who frequent the psychoanalyst's couch.

Other important aspects of Freud's work, however, have been qualified by subsequent research and have given way to new insights developed by psychologists who remain within the broad Freudian tradition. Perhaps best known of these "neo-Freudians" is Erik Erikson, whose sketch of eight stages of affective development is well known today.[8]

What Erikson's scheme does is extend the dialectical understanding of the personality into the realm of the emotions. It is important to realize, however, that like Piaget's concept of "equilibration" Erikson's understanding of emotional balance is that it is dynamic and not static. Growth is fostered by tension, not by the absence of tension. Erikson sees the dialectic at work in the continuing effort to balance trust with mistrust, autonomy with feelings of shame and doubt, initiative with guilt, industry with inferiority, a sense of identity with identity confusion, feelings of intimacy with feelings of isolation, generativity with stagnation, and wisdom with despair. Erikson's psychology is a good illustration of how progress towards affective maturity is made only by managing to retain and balance the opposites. A common misunderstanding, especially in religious applications of Erikson's theory, is to focus on the positive side of the dialectic at the expense of the negative pole. When that happens, tension is lost and development is hindered. Erikson's point, on the contrary, is that a certain amount of mistrust, identity confusion, and so forth is integral to human development.

Analytical Psychology

The analytical psychology of Carl Gustav Jung is predicated upon the necessity of maintaining a healthy relationship between a person's conscious ego self and the forces of the unconscious.[9] For Jung the unconscious is not merely a repository of forgotten or repressed personal experiences; it represents, rather, the collective experience of the race—the collective unconscious—from which the growing child gradually emerges as it comes to self-awareness. But the formation of the ego is only a partial realization of the vast potential of the unconscious. It is the human task, especially in the second half of life, to come to acknowledge and relate to the larger self, the symbol of wholeness, which is the fruit of appropriating both one's conscious and unconscious dimensions.

Because the unconscious is precisely that—unconscious—one has to come to terms with the symbolic images in which, through dreams and works of creative imagination, its various dynamics become available to consciousness. Thus there is a primary dialectic involved in the mutual relationship of one's conscious life and one's unconscious life. For the unconscious is, in Jung's view, alive and full of vitality. Just as our bodiliness roots our consciousness in the life of the body with its drives and instincts, so the life of the spirit is rooted deep in the energies and patterns of the unconscious, in the archetypes or basic patterns of perception. These too have a dialectical character: male/female, persona/shadow, anima/animus, *senex/puer*, life-giving mother/devouring mother. The process which Jung calls individuation or the journey towards wholeness is a process whereby the narrow and self-justifying ego consciousness gradually learns to serve the purposes of the larger self, being led by it to new and fuller life. For most of humanity, according to Jung, this process is accomplished through religious myths and rituals, which are projections or symbols of the numinous mystery into union with which we are called. Jung regarded his own psychological theory and its corresponding practices such as active imagination to be something made necessary in the West by the widespread collapse of religious belief and confidence in traditional religious symbols. But whether it is done through religion, as in Julian of Norwich's "oning" of the soul with God, or whether it is done through the struggle of psychoanalysis, the journey must be made, the paradoxes of life must be confronted, and the union or "coincidence of opposites" remains the goal of human life. The lotus, the beautiful flower which can only survive because its roots are sunk deep in the murky waters, is a symbol of this goal. We can become what we are called to be as human beings only if we sink our roots into the shadow side of our existence, into the depths of that larger self we all too easily ignore. More forcefully and certainly more poetically than anyone else Jung argued the inescapability of paradox, the necessity of dialectic, and the need to recognize the existence of opposing forces in human life. Without relating to those opposites, Jung showed that there can be no growth but only destruction, for what is denied entry into life through conscious recognition will subvert and destroy the house of consciousness.

Other Schools of Thought

Our purpose here is not so much to present contemporary theories of how the personality works, but simply to make as strongly as possible the point that the element of paradox and dialectic is basic to human life and growth and must therefore be given pride of place in our understanding of initiation. To indicate that the same dialectical principle is accepted across a wide variety of research areas, let us briefly mention two other fields in which this phenomenon has been identified.

The psychology of advertising is based on a great deal of empirical research into what attracts and holds people's attention. But it has also profited from research into the functions of the two sides of the brain which appear to act in complementary or dialectical fashion.[10] Though it is far from clear how the respective functions of the right and left sides of the brain can be clearly differentiated, it does seem to be the case that human behavior is motivated by forces of which the agent need not be at all conscious.[11] The importance of this for advertising, of course, is that products can be sold by subliminal messages, which can motivate a person to make a purchase without the buyer being conscious either of the motivation or of its source.

To turn lastly to quite a different field, the cultural anthropologist Victor Turner has developed the earlier "rites of passage" model, proposed in 1909 by the French anthropologist Arnold van Gennep, in a way which suggests that the social order itself and not merely the individual personality is constructed out of the tension created between opposing forces.[12] In this instance the opposing forces are what Turner calls "structure" and "antistructure." By social structure Turner means the whole hierarchical ordering and networking which characterizes established societies with their differentiations of rank, wealth, status, and so forth, and their organization of labor, education, and authority to functional ends. In short, structure is society as we know it most of the time. But there is another side to human beings which can never be entirely content with "structure," which yearns for a simpler, more immediate, more intimate and egalitarian way of relating, and this is what Turner calls *communitas* or "antistructure."

It is obviously impossible to spell out this theory in detail or to look at the evidence which Turner adduces in support of his views. What is important from our point of view is to see that here we have once again two sets of opposing forces which would seem to negate one another: structure/antistructure, hierarchy/equality, social distinctions/negation of social distinctions, and so forth. Yet it is Turner's conclusion that, for all their opposition, neither can survive without the other. Structure needs to remember its roots in the human yearning for the freedom and intimacy of *communitas*, but *communitas* cannot survive without becoming routine, ordered, structured—in short institutionalized. Both are in tension with one another, but if one should ever win out, the result would be either chaos or sterility.

DIALECTIC: A POSITIVE DYNAMIC WITHIN THE COMMUNITY

The purpose of citing all these examples of clinical, experimental, and anthropological research is simply to demonstrate that personal growth and even community vitality are not the products of simple, harmonious development, but the fruits of tension created by opposing tendencies. Most of the work we have referred to has evolved out of what was at first a conflictual approach to psychology, best exemplified in Freud's theory of the personality. For Freud, influenced by a Darwinian model of evolution as the survival of the fittest at the expense of the weakest, the individual ego was the result of a remorseless battle between the lawless energies of our animal instincts (the id) and the stern constraints imposed by internalized social authority (the superego). It took decades before Erikson, for example, was able to interpret the emergence of the ego in terms of a more positive dialectical interaction between self and culture. Likewise it has taken a generation or more before it came to be seen that Jungian psychology was less of an individual psychology than it was a social psychology, a way of understanding the individual's untapped potential against the background of the experience of countless generations of human beings and their accumulated wisdom.

What can we learn from this, and how does it relate to initiation? The overall conviction to which all these different authors lead us is that dialectic—tension created by opposing yet complementary forces—is to be sought not merely *within* the individual person, but most especially *between* self and society, individual and culture, person and community. In other words the best application of the dialectical principle is to see it at work in the way an individual interacts with the broader social and cultural systems of which that individual is a part.

Since we described initiation as the process of handing on the culture of a society to individual newcomers, the importance of a dialectical understanding of the relationship between individual and community is plain to see. If we are to reconsider and re-vision the event and process of initiation, we shall have to be particularly attentive to those areas in which this dialectic may show up: in the relationship of process to event, during the process of initiation itself, in the rites of initiation, in the subsequent follow-through, in the scriptural and liturgical images that guide initiation, in interpersonal relationships, and so forth.

The question of dialectic becomes particularly interesting when applied to liturgical rites. How might it be expressed in the symbolisms of the rite? How would our understanding of the necessity of dialectic affect the ways in which God is addressed or spoken of? How should the rite make manifest not only the numinous but also the demonic? How much should be made explicit to reason, how much left to unconscious intuition? How should the relationship between the "structure" of the Church community and the "anti-structure" of profound conversion be expressed? How are both the adulthood and the childhood of the community to be represented in the rites?

Since our task is not to answer such questions so much as to raise them, we shall be content to draw together material from the social sciences which relate to initiation under seven headings or principles. Nevertheless, in each of these principles, as will become evident, the same assumption is at work: growth in the individual and in the community is strongly influenced by how they hold in tension the opposing forces of the dialectic.

The dialectic at work in the first principle is one which pits the momentary event against the ongoing process in the task of initiation. Subsequent principles will identify tensions between the individual and the community (Principle II), the role of emotional patterns in the nuclear family (Principle III), the impact of the family's world view and interaction patterns on the process of initiation (Principle IV), the individual's trust and mistrust of others (Principle V), the need to adapt and reconcile conflicting world views (Principle VI), and the community's level of hospitality, shared affection, responsibility, and mission (Principle VII). Having argued that religious initiation can legitimately be regarded as a form of socialization and having shown some of the ways in which a dialectical movement is seen to pervade human development, it is now time to turn to the specific principles, which it is hoped will lead to a deeper understanding of the dynamics of initiation.

Part Two: Seven Principles Governing the Initiation Process

PRINCIPLE ONE: *Initiation is both an event and a gradual, developmental process by means of which the individual is socialized into the community.*

Initiation, as already noted, is being used here in the broadest sense of that term: to denote the welcoming of an individual into the religious culture of the community. It is, as we saw, a form of socialization and shares many of the characteristics of the process of socialization. This perspective contrasts with that in which baptism is usually discussed, for the focus of attention there is on the rite of baptism, the liturgical *event.* In fact, however, initiation, including Christian initiation, has two different, though inseparable dimensions: the process itself and the rites which accompany it, foster it, and to some extent accomplish it. Thus this first principle calls attention to the need to acknowledge both aspects and to try to understand the relationship between them.

The term initiation, of course, while not entirely without precedent in the history of Christian theology, derives today from anthropology and its studies of the process and ritualization of social incorporation among premodern cultures.[13] To someone unfamiliar with the total cultural and social context of the initiation rituals studied by anthropologists, it might appear that initiation rites are simply wonderfully colorful ceremonies, overlooking the significant preparation and follow-through which accompany them. Anthropological studies of initiation, however, such as those by Victor Turner, show that initiation is always a gradual and more or less lengthy process, not restricted to the ritual moments, though these ritual moments are often spread out over a long period and may even last several days at a time. However protracted the events, the process is nonetheless not simply coterminous with them.

If anthropological studies inevitably highlight the ritual dimensions of initiation, studies in genetic epistemology—how people come to know—underline the process dimension.

How do we know things? A common misunderstanding is to

think of knowing as being like looking: you know what your senses tell you is there to be known. This is what Bernard Lonergan calls "naive realism," and it supposes a clear differentiation between subject and object, between the knower and what is known. However commonsensical such an understanding of the act of knowing might seem, the research of people like Jean Piaget in cognitive development have provided ample evidence that knowledge is not simply received, as if into an empty vessel, but is in fact filtered by patterns of perception and mental frameworks. To know then is not merely to receive sense data, but to process that data, to work on it, and to construct meaning out of it. The knower does not merely receive information from the environment, but actively processes that information in order to understand and respond to the environment.

When we think of initiation as the handing on of a culture, it becomes obvious that such handing on is not simply a matter of those who know depositing information in the empty minds of those who are ignorant. Meanings and values cannot be transferred like objects from one generation to the next. Rather, the next generation—or the individual who represents it—works it over, assimilates it, and makes it its own. Hence we have the dialectic we have so much insisted upon, one between self and society, and meaning is constructed by the individual in an ongoing balancing act. Knowledge, according to Piaget, is not held in random piles, but stored in patterns. When new information comes along, the individual either finds a place for it within his existing patterns of knowing or else has to rearrange the framework of his thinking and valuing to accommodate the new. In this way the internal structure or patterns already constructed by the individual on the basis of past experience or knowledge are adjusted continually to new experiences of knowing.[14]

This confirms our claim that initiation must be a process and not merely an event, for it takes time to assimilate new knowledge and experience and to restructure one's ways of thinking and valuing. But it also suggests something further, namely, that initiation is a process not only for the candidates themselves but also for those associated with them in the initiating community. For socialization continues not only for youths but for adults as well, and not only for the baptized but for the family and friends of the baptized and for the entire parish.

When we consider the other principles, we shall discuss various aspects of the process not only as it affects the candidate for baptism but others as well. But initially it is important to make the following points: initiation is both event and process; the individual is not passive in undergoing initiation but actively assimilates the new in his or her own way; initiation is a process of socialization not only for the individual but also for the community. These important facts are all the more likely to be overlooked when the candidate for the rites of initiation is a newborn child. Here the temptation is to focus on the baptismal event and let the process take care of itself or to think that everything that has to do with baptism happens during the ceremony. That is a dangerous temptation, and everything in these pages is directed to overcoming the impression that the baptismal rite takes place in isolation, that it only affects the child, and that the child is purely passive. The baptismal event, it should become clear, is an event in the life of the child and one to which it may well be important for the grown or growing person to be able to look back. But it is also a significant event in the life of the family and in the life of the Church (parish). Both children and adults, if they are to grow into their religious culture, must continue to construct and reconstruct the values and meanings that belong to that culture. Knowledge—even Christian knowledge—is less a reified set of static truths that someone may be said to "have" than a kind of "know-how" which deepens and grows as life goes on.

Thus in baptism the child is not purely passive, nor the adult community purely active. The child is already acting upon them and has been perhaps since the time of its conception, if not long before. The community has to adjust to it in so many ways. The process of initiation is thus a reciprocal learning process in which the child is introduced to the community and culture of faith and also makes a contribution by its very presence. In the event of baptism, all these processes are at work and need to be attended to.

Questions: How does the ritual event—or events—fit into the process of socialization when the event is considered from the child's vantage point? In what perceptible ways does this child presented for baptism challenge and stretch the habitual ways of thinking and living adopted by its family and by the wider community? Where does the ritual event fit into the ongoing socialization of the child's family and of the wider community?

PRINCIPLE TWO: *Initiation is a process by which the individual and the community mutually construct their shared values and identity.*

Although socialization theory in general describes the whole process by which shared values are communicated between generations, researchers have given particular attention to the relationship between parents and their teenage children. Findings have demonstrated that parents play a central role in shaping the values of young people.[15] Nevertheless, the empirical sciences have not progressed to the point of being able to measure exactly which persons or groups are the most influential forces in the socialization process. For this reason we shall be content here to indicate the consensus that does exist that parents are indeed among the most important influences upon the cultural assimilation or socialization of their children.

The influence of parents upon the emotional patterns of their childrens' lives has been affirmed by clinicians such as Bruno Bettelheim working with clients in psychotherapy.[16] Study of the values held by young people points to the same conclusions. A recently completed analysis of survey responses from six thousand youths indicates that the strongest predictor of the extent of a young person's religious socialization (that is, their engagement in prayer and sacraments and their avoidance of drugs and sex) is the extent to which he or she is able to talk with their parents about moral and religious matters.[17] Working with much younger children, Marian Radke Yarrow of the National Institute of Health has confirmed that among preschool children the way a child responds to seeing others in need is closely associated with certain parenting patterns.[18]

From a different but as we shall see highly significant perspective, the central role of parents in the development of their children is strongly confirmed by the research of family systems therapists, who look at their clients not as isolated individuals with isolated problems but as members of a family. It is above all to the constellation of family relationships that family systems therapists look for the source and the solution of their clients' problems.[19]

The approach of family systems theory corresponds closely to the direction of empirical studies of socialization in the last twenty years. Earlier forms of socialization theory were characterized by two features which have been progressively abandoned in recent years. First, they tended to think of the person being socialized as being essentially passive under the process. Second, they tended to focus on the psychological stage of the recipient to the exclusion of the psychological stages of the major participants in that person's socialization, such as parents and siblings or other significant adults. At the present time socialization, the assimilation of meanings and values, is looked at from a life cycle approach. That is to say, the stage of the child's development is looked at in conjunction with where the parents "are at" psychologically and developmentally. Sonya L. Rhodes, one of the earliest researchers to develop this dynamic approach to child development, has proposed five stages of family growth, each stage coordinated to where the parents and children are at any given moment in terms of Erik Erikson's eight stages.[20]

All these different kinds of research shed light on the interaction between the individual and the community and highlight the importance of the parents' role. A distinct shift is occurring in this research and practice, from an exclusive focus on the individual to a broader perspective on the way the family as a whole operates. In this broader perspective one would hope that more light will be shed on how the individual influences the family system, but in the present state of research, more information is available on how the family influences the individual. In what follows there will be hints on how the individual might be seen to be influencing the community in important ways, but since we are summarizing existing research, the emphasis will have to be on the community's role in shaping the individual in the process of initiation.

Earlier forms of research tended to accord so much importance to the community as to make the individual appear a merely passive recipient of its meanings and values. As could be expected, this research led to the development of similarly one-sided approaches to such practical matters as education, parenting, and moral development. We in contrast shall try to reflect the contemporary understanding of socialization as an interactive, reciprocally influential process. Not only are parents' values, for example, to be seen as constitutive of the family and therefore of the child's values,[21] but the adults must also be seen as likely to have to change when confronted with the challenges raised by their children.[22]

Moreover much of the work done on the transmission of values tends to focus inevitably on parents with children in their teenage years, when the issue of values becomes particularly acute. Our perspective, however, is that of younger parents with newborn or newly adopted children whom they are presenting for baptism. The question of the parents' values (intentionality) is equally critical when the child first comes upon the scene and breaks into their lives. Specifically looking at the family as a total system or a group of people, who together and not just as individuals contribute to the life of the Church and require pastoral care, has direct implications for the event of baptism and for the more comprehensive process of initiation or religious socialization. Since it is not the task of this chapter to explore those implications, perhaps we can end this section with some questions which point in that direction.

> *Questions:* How do the parents see their role in the ongoing Christian initiation of their children?
>
> What can be discovered about the parents' acknowledged or unacknowledged attitudes towards their children which will shape those children in significant ways?
>
> How do the liturgies of Christian initiation acknowledge and shape the role of the parents vis-à-vis their children and vis-à-vis the Church?

PRINCIPLE THREE: *The emotional patterns of the initiate's nuclear and extended family are central—if not dominant—forces influencing the meaning of the ritual event and the process of initiation.*

This principle calls attention to a factor too often overlooked in thinking about the sacrament of baptism and the initiation process of which the sacrament is a part, namely, the kinds of relationships and the patterns of relationship that exist in the family and circle of the initiate—in our case the child presented for baptism. We here take up the matter of the reciprocal influence exerted both by the individual and by the family upon each other, exploring it in terms of the patterns of interaction that characterize a particular family. In other words, instead of seeing the family as a collection of individuals of whom the newborn baby is the most passive, it looks at the whole family as a system of active relationships.

The shift from focussing on the parts to studying the whole system which characterizes what is called "systems theory" can be exemplified by thinking of an automobile and how it is built.[23] A traditional analytic approach to studying a problem would be represented by a manufacturer inviting a hundred top engineers to examine a hundred top automobiles and by selecting the best parts of each car—carburetor, brakes, shock absorbers, and so forth—

to build the perfect car. The process would clearly not work because the parts would not be compatible with each other. The parts of a car do not exist by themselves but as parts of a larger entity—or system—the car for which they were made. General systems theory, in contrast, begins with the assumption that the best car is the car whose parts work together the best. This is a synthetic rather than an analytic approach, and its goal is to articulate the principles governing the interaction of the parts. Parts are not considered in themselves but only as parts of a larger system.

Another example might be a university. A traditional analytic approach would see a university in terms of all the individual schools and departments that are found there. By contrast, a systems approach looks at the entire university and the way it operates as a whole to prepare its students for life ahead. While the traditional approach would analyze the university into its constituent parts, the systems approach would try to understand how the university works by considering how it interacts with the larger social and educational system.

The beginnings of modern systems theory are usually traced to a series of presentations given by Ludwig von Bertanlaffy to the Charles Morris Philosophy Seminar at the University of Chicago in 1937.[24] Von Bertanlaffy himself came to develop this approach from his background in biology. But there were other thinkers—Norbert Wiener in cybernetics, W. Kohler in gestalt psychology, A. N. Whitehead in philosophy, and Kurt Goldstein in psychiatry—who were coming to much the same convictions in their own fields.[25] Most of them would have felt comfortable with von Bertanlaffy's definition of a system: "Any organism is a system, that is, a dynamic order of parts and processes (components) standing in mutual interaction."[26] There are in fact two sets of interactions going on in an organism: the interaction of the parts of the organism among themselves and the interaction of the whole organism with its environment.

It is clearly helpful to think of the family as such an organism and of the individual as part of a family system, which as a family interacts with the wider community in certain characteristic ways. Clearly, too, this acknowledgement has pastoral implications, not least when a family presents a child for baptism. It therefore seems worthwhile to explore the family as a system, and we shall do that first by giving four basic principles of general systems theory and then by applying those principles to the family. This should shed light on initiation, which by any definition involves the integration of a new member into an existing system, whether it be that of the family or that of the Church community.

Four basic principles of general systems theory may be briefly stated as follows.

First, to understand an organism, whether that organism be a physical or a social entity, it is necessary to understand how it is organized. "We cannot speak of living things or of their behavior without taking account of their organization."[27]

Second, a system may be said to be "open" to the extent that it is able to exchange matter, energy, or information with its environment. Such openness, it is to be noted, is as necessary for the survival of a social system (for example, a family or parish) as it is for the survival of a physical system (for example, a plant).

Third, the extent of a system's openness is largely determined by the characteristic features of its boundaries. "The boundary of a system, it has been said, is that region separating one system from another whose function is to filter or select inputs and outputs."[28] Every system has its limits—its skin, its parameters, its edges— through which matter, energy, and information go to and fro, enabling the system to function. One thinks of the human body, with its senses and its orifices, or the human mind in constant interaction with the world around it. But selectivity is the key factor, the ability to filter what goes in and out.

Fourth, systems tend to maintain a certain constancy or stability in relation to their environment. But it is important not to be misled by the terms constancy and stability: there is nothing static about a system's interaction with its environment. Rather it is characterized by constant disequilibrium, an ongoing series of adjustments to change, and to the new elements entering or leaving the system. A simple example of this would be the thermostat. Through the thermostat the home's heating system constantly interacts with rising or falling temperatures outside the home.[29]

These four principles can be directly applied to the family unit considered as a system.

A family is only understood when the way that family organizes itself is understood. Elements in the organization of a given family would include the way the family members interact with each other as well as the rules and policies, whether explicit or implicit, under which the family operates.

For a family to be able to maintain itself, there needs to be a certain amount of give and take with the larger society, that is, a certain amount of matter, energy, and information need to flow into and out of the family. In short the family needs both to draw upon the wider community and to contribute to it. It needs to interact with the world outside the home.

The boundary of a family is determined by how the family in question defines itself and how the individual members of that family define themselves in relation to the family as a whole. In a healthy family there are boundaries which could be said to be semipermeable, that is, sufficiently closed for the family to have its own clear and unique identity but at the same time sufficiently open to admit new information and new people and to be able to adapt to its changing environment. The individual whose identity is characterized by a similar semipermeability is one whom Murray Bowen has called self-differentiated.[30] Bowen cites the example of the salmon prepared if need be to swim against the current. On the other hand, if boundaries are too closed or too open, too rigid or too adaptable, the family or the individual will become dysfunctional. For such a state Bowen uses the image of the jellyfish, carried to and fro by the tide. A fine characterization of the family whose system really works is that given by Herbert Anderson, who describes the goal of family life as one of enabling people "to be separate together."[31] That summarizes pretty well what is meant here by boundaries in the family system.

The fourth principle, that of homeostatic equilibrium, is exemplified by G. K. Chesterton's remark that our forward progress is dependent upon our lurching from imbalance to imbalance. Where the family is concerned, this principle draws our attention to how the family copes with change, for example, the arrival of a new child. The health of a family is largely determined by its adaptive capacities, while the health of the family as a whole is critically important for the health of its individual members. The ability to cope with the new and continually to adapt without losing its own identity is crucial for the family and its members.

What implications does thinking of the family as a system have for the understanding of initiation as a process and for the celebration of the rituals of initiation?

Rabbi Edwin Friedman, a noted therapist as well as a pastor, has roundly criticized social scientists for tending to focus in their studies of religious rituals either on the religious community as a whole or on the individual undergoing the ritual. Either way, he points out, the role of the family is ignored.[32] The parallel with the theological attention paid to the minister of the sacrament (variously seen as the priest or the community as a whole) and to the subject or recipient of the sacrament is obvious. Nonetheless, speaking from twenty years' experience as a clergyman and as a therapist, Friedman concludes that "the family, far from being an intermediary, is the primary force operating at such moments—primary not only in that it, and not the culture, determines the emotional quality of such occasions (and therefore the success of the passage), but also in that it is the family more than the culture which determines which rites are to be used."[33]

To put this another way, we might say that it is the family as well as the individual that is going through a transition in times of birth, death, or marriage. Moreover the ceremony and associated processes engage not merely the individual in relation to the family but also the family in relation to the wider community, for example, the parish. Even more, to the degree that the broader community is actually involved in the process and in the rites, then the broader community too will be to some extent "in transition." Thus from a systems point of view, the attention so often paid to historical, theological, denominational, and cultural variables associated with the rite is at the expense of paying attention to the unseen and unexamined family process dynamics that are at work as people interact with each other during the process leading up to the ritual event. Friedman pulls no punches in saying what he thinks of this state of affairs when he writes that contemporary "medicine men for all their hocus-pocus have only succeeded in driving the spooks and spirits further from view, just making them, therefore, harder to exorcise or control."[34] An example of this would be a wedding where all the fussy attention to the details of the celebration may only serve to mask a highly important family process—such as the parents' pain at losing their child—which is going on all the while. From a systems perspective it is important that such a parent pay attention not only to their separation from their child but also to their own experience of separating from their own parents. This is not likely to happen, because contemporary religious wedding rites minimize the central role of the families of origin. As a result the parent tends to take it out on the new and culturally different son- or daughter-in-law. So the ghost slips through to haunt a new generation.

What "spooks and spirits" might be hidden from view by the

fuss surrounding the celebration of baptism? Encouragement to take this question seriously comes from an interestingly different quarter, the Counter-Reformation studies of historian John Bossy. The sixteenth and seventeenth-century Catholic reform movement led to the adoption of policies, Bossy demonstrates, which exalted the importance of the institution, whether it be the local bishop or the local parish, at the expense of the role of the family in the life of the Church. What made this—and continues to make this—particularly difficult to deal with is that the family is not explicitly discounted; it is merely totally ignored in the development of public policy. This means that the devaluation of the family was never publicly discussed and thus became a hidden liability passed on from generation to generation and never adequately exorcised.[35] Perhaps the exorcism has now finally begun to happen, for Pope John Paul II has ordered that no new Church programs or policies should be initiated without there first being an assessment of their potential impact upon families and family life.[36]

In summary, then, a systems point of view would suggest that any "re-visioning" of Christian initiation will benefit from a review of how sacramental policies look when seen in light of the possibility that it is not the individual, not the local community, not the whole Catholic culture, but the emotional and behavioral patterns of the family that are the most significant factors both in the process of initiation and in the celebration of the rites.

> *Questions:* How early in the process—that is, how long before the celebration of baptism—should the (prospective) parents be encouraged to reflect upon their family-as-system?
>
> What sort of "spooks and spirits" might be hidden by a baptismal celebration and baptismal preparation that focuses on doctrine or on ceremonial minutiae and avoids raising questions about the family system and how it is coping (or going to cope) with the new child?
>
> What traditional ritual elements lend themselves to making explicit the role of the family, especially the parents, in Christian initiation?

PRINCIPLE FOUR: *The individual's capacity for participating in the event and process of initiation depends upon certain fundamental adaptive capabilities learned in the person's family of origin.*

It should be clear by now that we are dealing with initiation as a total process which the ritual event celebrates. In saying that the ritual *celebrates* the process, we are suggesting that the verbal stories and images portrayed in the rite, together with the nonverbal symbols such as time, place, roles, movements, and gestures and symbolic objects like water, font, and altar, project a specific world view (the Christian faith) and rehearse the participants in attitudes and commitments which are consonant with such a world view. In saying that the rite celebrates the *total* process, we are implying that baptism cannot be understood as something that only happens to the baptized infant but that initiation affects the views and commitments of others besides the child. Since in fact the full initiation of the child only occurs in interaction with the community of believers—most immediately the family—the other members of the family, together with whatever broader circle of friends and parishioners may be involved, are all liable to have their own outlooks, understandings, and values called into question by the rite and reshaped by the process. Baptism is not only for the child; it is for the Church, and especially it is for the particular Church (that is family and local community) which is drawn into this child's baptism and initiation. This fourth principle, together with the remaining principles that follow, spells out the implications of this systems perspective.

An individual is only capable of sharing the community's world view to the degree that he or she is capable of perceiving patterns of meaning. But this capacity to perceive patterns of meaning is a skill learned in one's family of origin. Family life in short largely shapes the way an individual perceives reality. Sigmund Freud argued that this was true of children's attitudes toward authority and toward sexuality, but therapists since then have come to refine this basic insight and to identify more, and more specific, ways in which parental attitudes shape the personalities of their children.

One particular study is especially interesting for the insights it offers into how personality factors affect that process of mutual influence which we have been calling initiation. David Reiss, Director of the Center for Family Research at the George Washington School of Medicine in Washington, D.C., has studied how interpersonal dynamics in a family are tied up with the world view of the family members and with their ability to adapt and change.[37] Looking at how a family interacts with its environment, Reiss studied the ways in which different families worked together when confronted with an abstract puzzle provided by the researchers. The result of this rather unique approach to studying the family was much greater understanding of the ways in which the world view of family members was influenced by the relationships between parents and children.

Reiss began with the hypothesis that if individuals can hold myths—that is, "constructs of what was the real world"—then it was possible that families too hold myths. The study itself, based on family systems theory such as I have described above, began in 1967 by comparing dysfunctional families, including schizophrenic families, with "normal" families who had no unusual problems and who were recruited from local parent teacher associations. This early stage of the research succeeded in identifying three types of families according to how they approach the task of solving the puzzle.

The first group consisted of the severely dysfunctional families. Their approach to problem-solving was to form a united front against others, to obtain a quick consensus on a solution, and to sacrifice the complexity of the problem in favor of a feeling of family solidarity. In so doing they ignored some of the clues. Reiss also noted that such families were suspicious of the researchers. The second group was composed of families who had one member suffering from some sort of personality disorder. Unlike the first group the researchers found this family type did not function as a unit. Instead, each family member operated alone. The third group of families, all of the "normal" kind, approached the problem-solving task by working together, following all the clues, listening to each other's suggestions, and regarding the whole exercise as a game they were happy to play.

Since that early research the same methods have been used in studying several hundred middle class families, only to confirm the same three types of family as were identified in 1967. It was found moreover that some functioning families who had never sought clinical help in fact adopted ways of solving the puzzle similar to the approach attributed above to the severely dysfunctional families. This finding had no negative connotations for Reiss, since each of the three approaches has something to commend it.[38] But what is important to bear in mind is that these three types of families are characterized not only by the patterns of interaction specific to each but also by the family myth or outlook which renders the members of the family more or less adaptable to change—and thus from our perspective more or less open to the process of initiation. Since these three approaches are likely to be met within the process of initiation, it might be well to say a little more about each of them.

The first type of family, known as "consensus sensitive," manages to achieve a united front but at the cost of avoiding conflict among themselves. As a result they do poorly when it comes to solving problems, since they are more preoccupied with maintaining family unity than with handling things that affect them from outside. In sum they are high on coordination, sharing the same world view, but score low on configuration, since they are rather slow to recognize patterns and have little mastery of their social environment.

The second family type, known as "interpersonal-distance sensitive," does not work well together. Its members tend to be individualists and to be caught up in competition between each other so that they ignore each other's solutions. Thus they score low on coordination because their world views do not mesh, but they also score low on configuration, since they too are slow to recognize patterns and have little sense of control over their environment. They are somewhat turned in on each other, but competitively rather than cooperatively.

The third type is known as "environment-sensitive." These are families who recognize that the problem is "out there" in the social environment and do not turn it into a problem within the family. Members tend to believe that the solution to such problems can be arrived at by logical thinking and by joint effort. Since they do not take the problem to heart, they enjoy working with the clues and coming to a solution. Such families score high on coordination, since they share the same outlook, and they also score high on configuration, because they succeed in recognizing patterns and are confident in dealing with the outside world.

The purpose of describing this study by Reiss is to indicate that there are solid empirical reasons for thinking that the world view of a particular family is closely associated with how the family members interact among themselves, with their extended family, circle of friends, and the wider society, including the parish. This study also provides categories with which to describe how individuals interact with others in terms of their world view. In other words, whether an individual is able to adapt to change will largely be determined by the patterns of relating he or she has learned, usually quite unconsciously, in the family in which he or she grew up. Because all the members of the same family tend to adopt the same outlook and to act in similar ways, they tend to relate to people outside the family in the same characteristic pattern. This shared approach to outsiders in fact acts as a paradigm for their world view: behavioral patterns are accompanied by characteristic and ongoing assumptions about what the world is like. Of course this world view is seldom something consciously articulated, but it nonetheless pervades a family's relationship with its social environment, including its relationship to matters of faith and the local religious community.

To understand this better, it will be necessary to elaborate a little on what is meant by configuration and coordination, while introducing yet a third term, closure.[39] Configuration refers to the capacity of the individual and the family to recognize patterns. For example it includes the ability of individual members to find their place in the extended family network without losing the ability to function autonomously. It is also associated with members' self-confidence when it comes to dealing with the larger social world. Families that function well tend to score high on configuration. Coordination, on the other hand, is a matter of the individual being able to fit his or her own vision and problem-solving efforts into the larger process of family living. A highly coordinated family is one whose members have a strong sense of the family as a unit and realize that what happens to one member will affect all the others. Finally, closure is the ability to postpone a final decision until all the evidence is in. The ability to live with uncertainty until a decision is ready to be taken is referred to as high closure and is the opposite of compulsive rushing to conclusions and decisions.

The thesis here is that each of these three capacities are important both for the process of initiation and for the ritual event. The message presented to the initiate by the community, for example, implies that the world is indeed an ordered world, that life is intelligible and can be taken on with confidence. The Christian message which conveys such convictions is marked by a more or less high degree of configuration. Similarly the new member has to learn that we are all members of one body, that the life and death of each of us affects and is affected by the other members. This is what we have called coordination. Finally the ability to postpone a decision until all relevant information is available—to live with what Roger Schutz has called "the power of the provisional"—is what is required by a life of ongoing conversion and continuing discovery. For people with high closure, the Christian life is a journey of faith rather than a static possession of truth. So the commitment of such people is deep and firm, but not close-minded.

What these empirical studies and their threefold description of the capacity for adaptation have in common with initiation is their association with myth. In other words, the process of initiation and the capacity of families and family members to adapt to changes in their world both depend heavily upon the possession of a holistic vision of the world and of one's relationship to it. This suggests that liturgists and pastoral ministers would be well advised to look carefully at the myths represented in the rites of initiation to see whether and how they might foster what we have called high configuration, high coordination, and high closure among the initiates. Moreover in serving a specific community or a specific family through the long process of initiation, it may prove very fruitful to explore the myths, outlooks, and world views operative within that community or family, to see whether they encourage or discourage people's adaptive capabilities. Particularly crucial will be the way in which the parents and family of a child presented for baptism conceive of their world and relate to the larger world, for it is the family's adaptive ability which will largely shape, in the long term, the child's ability to adapt, to change, and to be converted to a more wholehearted and committed life of faith.

In fact the arrival of a new child is a fundamental challenge to the outlook and relational patterns of a family. The addition of one new person requires that everyone else adjust. How a family adjusts to this and other subsequent changes and how it understands what is going on are critical to the health both of the family and of the child. It is critical, too, to the quality of its faith life. Perhaps the rite of baptism can serve as a stabilizing ritual in the midst of a destabilizing period of adjustment. It can be stabilizing, not in the sense of offering false comfort or false security, but in the sense that it acknowledges the negative aspects of the process as well as the positive. The ritual subsumes both aspects into a larger, archetypal pattern, which assures believers that this is as it should be and that the same pattern of confronting change with shared faith and hope lies at the heart of the Christian Gospel.

Questions: How does the parish as a whole and the pastoral team in particular handle change? If the parish is considered an extended family or the pastoral staff as a nuclear family, how do they score on configuration, coordination, and closure?

How do the considerations offered under this fourth principle affect pastoral strategy towards families seeking the baptism of their children? Specifically, given that the Church requires assurances that the child will in fact be brought up as a believer, how do these considerations relate to the criteria invoked in deciding whether or not to baptize a child?

PRINCIPLE FIVE: *The level of trust which participants bring to the event and process of ritualization is crucial for its outcome.*

In the wake of the Second World War, American social scientists began to search for whatever flaws or traits in human character might begin to suggest an explanation for the fact that a large number of otherwise apparently normal people, the Nazis, could coldly harness their technological prowess to the systematic murder of six million Jews. This study, intended to predict and prevent the recurrence of such a phenomenon, turned out to be the largest empirical research project ever undertaken. Its findings were published under the title *The Authoritarian Personality,*[40] a title which summarizes the project's conclusion that the monstrosity of National Socialism was the fruit of a tendency to surrender one's individuality to the domination of authority figures.

As it turned out, the testing instrument used—the so-called F-scale—proved to be seriously flawed in the way it was biased against conservative beliefs, so that this original study has now been overtaken by subsequent, more accurate research. Among second generation researchers into this problem, the name of Milton Rokeach, designer of the D-scale, is the most prominent. Rokeach's work has demonstrated that we do not just hold beliefs, but that our beliefs interact with one another. It is not so much *what* is believed but *how* a person believes that characterizes the dogmatic personality.[41]

Rokeach's further research investigated the relative importance of the different beliefs in a person's belief system and showed that a distinction needs to be made between what he called "central," "intermediate," and "peripheral" beliefs.[42] The difference between these three categories of belief can be illustrated with reference to the following diagram:

1	peripheral beliefs
2 3	
4 5 6	intermediate beliefs
7 8 9 10	
11 12 13 14 15	central beliefs

A person's central beliefs are those which, when altered, inevitably provoke a realignment of the rest of a persons' beliefs. They are represented in the chart by blocks 12, 13, and 14. At the opposite extreme are the purely peripheral beliefs, represented by blocks 1, 2, and 3. They can be dropped or modified without having any serious consequences for the individual's system of beliefs. Functionally they are the least important and are easily sacrificed. Between these two are beliefs that are more or less important, represented by blocks 4 through 10, in the intermediate category. These are the sort of beliefs that carry more weight than a person's purely peripheral beliefs, yet are not as basic to his or her belief system as some others, so their modification need not call the whole belief system into question.

What sort of beliefs are likely to prove central to a person's belief system? Reviewing the research and the theoretical literature pertaining to the issue, Rokeach concluded that *trust* was a major differentiating factor between open and closed minds. More specifically three kinds of trust are involved: psychological trust (trust in oneself); sociological trust (trust in others); and physiological trust (trust in one's physical environment).[43] This means that a person lacking confidence in his or her ability to understand what is going on and adequately to respond to it is unlikely to be receptive to new information. Instead, such persons will be preoccupied simply with filtering their daily experience for hints of reassurance concerning their self-worth. People who tend to be distrustful of others, on the other hand, will prefer to work alone and will not prove very cooperative. This creates social isolation, which in turn creates a barrier against the flow of information, affection, and other forms of mutual assistance and interaction. Finally a person distrustful of the physical world will not be inclined to take care of the environment and will draw no sustenance from it.

Conversely someone who has developed a healthy trust of self, others, and the world is likely to be open and nondogmatic in his or her beliefs. Rokeach has shown that there are empirical criteria by which to contrast open and closed belief systems and to measure how open or closed a person's mind might be. His whole approach is quite consistent with the sort of general systems theory outlined above and is in fact a particular application of that theory. However, it is easier to identify the negative than the positive aspects of a system, that is, to say what characterizes a closed mind rather than what constitutes an open one. So it is that on the basis of Rokeach's research and of hundreds of related studies using the D-scale, the following are commonly accepted as the characteristics of a closed mind: the tendency to keep apart beliefs which logically speaking should belong together; the tendency to indulge in global statements of opinion and belief without recognizing the need for nuance or the importance of making distinctions; the lack of a comprehensive synthesis of ideas; a tendency to relate to authority in ways which either exaggerate its importance or disregard its proper role; a tendency to live either in the past or in the present or else in the future, to the exclusion of the other two time modes.

In other words, bearing in mind the three different kinds of beliefs identified above, the closed mind works in clearly recognizable ways. It is inclined to treat the peripheral as if it were central and vice-versa; it holds contradictory beliefs without recognizing the need to resolve the contradiction; it lacks coherence in its thinking and believing; it either conforms to the teaching and directives of authority or else it has an exaggerated sense of its own authority; it is incapable of recognizing the importance of the temporal flow, of deciding the present in the light of the past in order to shape the future.

What makes all this of interest to our discussion of religious initiation of children is the further finding that the way parents organize their beliefs is passed on to their children. A study of five hundred families administered the Rokeach Dogmatism Scale to both parents and children and yielded convincing evidence that dogmatic parents tend to have dogmatic children while open-minded parents pass their open-mindedness on to their offspring. Similar studies have shown consistently strong correlations between parents and children on such basic personality traits as anxiety and anomie. Furthermore there are good reasons for thinking that broader aggregate groups, such as a church community or parish, will also be characterized by aggregate levels of closed-mindedness or open-mindedness, especially in regard to specific subjects such as social justice, sexuality, or biblical interpretation.

Can findings such as these shed any light upon the process of initiation or upon the rites of initiation? Can recognition of the patterns of open and closed belief systems enable those involved in initiation—not only the candidates but the family and the parish community—to be more open to the meaning of what is happening? This requires further discussion, but some preliminary remarks may help to indicate promising lines of reflection.

How people understand initiation and the sense they make of the rites are likely to be conditioned very largely by the degree to which they are open- or closed-minded. We saw, for example, that closed-minded people fail to see the logical connections and implications of the beliefs they hold. When it comes to initiation, then, such people are likely to see the rite of baptism as an isolated event, not connecting it with what leads up to the baptism nor to the ongoing initiation which follows baptism. They will also insist on thinking of baptism as being simply for the infant, failing to recognize its implications for the family and the broader community. The open mind, on the contrary, will make such connections. It will see the rite as taking up what has happened in the period before baptism and being in direct continuity with what happens in the follow-up to the rite. Critically important here, of course, is the mind-set of the pastor or pastoral staff. If those responsible for coordinating the rite with the pastoral work that precedes and follows it do not make the connections, the connections will not easily be made. This would be like a farmer sowing his fields without having ploughed them first or having made provision for harvesting: he would not be in business long.

Attitudes to authority are telltale clues to the open or closed belief system. These show up in initiation in various ways. The dogmatic frame of mind is exemplified by those who regard baptism as a legitimation of their own world view or who deny that anyone can be saved or win divine favor without going through the rite. Believers who are more characteristically open-minded can affirm the authoritative character of their own religious tradition and the importance of being initiated into it while still admitting the limitations inherent in the community's claim to know the truth and thus being open to the truth and value to be found in other systems or traditions. They do not find it necessary to claim possession of all truth in order to avoid sliding into a meaningless relativism.

Similar patterns are at work with participants' sense of time and history. Open-minded Christians, as opposed to dogmatists, will be concerned to build bridges between the child and the historical past, whether that of the family or of the Church. They will likewise have a lively awareness of what the child's and the world's future might bring, realizing the continuity between what is celebrated in baptism and what will unfold as the future itself unfolds.

All this, as we said at the beginning, has to do with the level of trust each of us has in three critical dimensions: trust in oneself, trust in others, trust in one's world. Erik Erikson has proposed that the infant's first task in life is that of learning to trust and that the capacity for trust is the root of religiosity. The trust levels of parents and parishioners are already largely conditioned by their own experience of life and by the ethos of the community to which they belong. But the arrival of new children and the assuming of responsibility for those children should provoke a coming-to-awareness of these dimensions of trust and of the relationship of these dimensions with God. Thus the celebration of baptism could be an occasion for identifying and reflecting upon the central beliefs in our individual and communal belief system: the trust we repose in ourselves, in our neighbor, and in the physical universe. Then the rite itself might need to include symbols that relate to such trust. Indeed there could hardly be a more powerful image of such threefold trust than the rite of immersion, a profound symbol upon which trust of self, trust of others, and trust of the physical world all converge and point beyond themselves to the God into whose love this candidate is committed. What this fifth principle points out, however, is that such trusting commitment cannot be made ritually and be effective unless it becomes a characteristic way of being in the world for parents and parish alike.

Questions: What sort of things would people look to in a family or parish if they wanted to tell whether their respective belief systems were open or closed?

Religious instruction, including prebaptismal preparation, is usually more concerned with *what* Christians believe than with *how* they believe. How could more attention be paid to the question of how we organize our beliefs and of what the implications of this might be?

How does religious ritual in general, and Christian initiation ritual in particular, foster either dogmatism or open-mindedness, low trust levels or high trust levels?

A recurring theme throughout these principles has been the issue of change and how individuals, parents, families, and parishes adjust to change. What religious/theological significance is to be attributed to that?

PRINCIPLE SIX: *The process of initiation presents an opportunity for the participants—parents, siblings, parish—to confront, adapt, and reconcile their disparate world views.*

The term Christian initiation is usually used to refer to something that happens at the baptism of children or of adult converts. Restricting the term to the rite itself, however, overlooks the significance of the rather serious adjustments that are being made at this time by the converts or, in the case of infant baptism, by the child's family. Often these periods of adjustment are sufficiently wrenching to deserve to be called crises. The question therefore arises of how people actually cope with such transitions.

One approach favored by some research into how individuals and families cope with the need to adjust to such changes is based on the early writings of John Dewey, writings which have also served educators and moral developmentalists as a guide in their attempts to elaborate what constitutes value.[44] Dewey sketched seven steps that individuals must take if they are really to appropriate their own experience. They are as follows: 1. seeing alternatives; 2. thinking about the alternatives; 3. being free of undue pressure to choose one alternative over the other; 4. deciding, or cherishing one of the alternatives; 5. articulating that choice verbally; 6. putting it into effect; and 7. continuing to do so over time. These seven steps actually involve three basic processes: seeing (1, 2, 3), judging (4), and acting (5, 6, 7). In times of stress, families instinctively go through some form of this process of seeing, judging, and acting, as they attempt to assess and adjust to their situation.[45]

David Reiss and Mary Oliveri[46] have further refined our understanding of how families adjust to change. Their research has identified three stages in the process: definition of the event or problem together with a search for additional information (seeing); initial responses and trial solutions (judging); and final decision (judging) or closing position (judging) together with the family's commitment (acting) to this decision or position. As one would expect from what we have seen of the need for a family to recognize patterns in the crisis, coordinate their vision or outlook, and come to closure on a strategy for handling it, each phase of adjustment will be strongly affected by the particular family's habits of thinking and acting (see Principle Five). In the "crisis" of Christian initiation, a family will have to move somehow through the stages of adjustment just described, but how it does so will depend upon the adjustive capacities it has as a family.

What this means in practice can be spelled out by looking at how the best-equipped families—those who score high on configuration, coordination, and closure—might be expected to handle the crisis of the arrival of a new child and its Christian initiation.

The Early Phase: Defining the Event

At this stage the family would engage in three sets of operations. First, it would assume responsibility for the event of the child's birth or adoption and for coping with the changes which this is inevitably to wreak in the family's existing patterns. This corresponds to what David Reiss calls configuration and is of great pastoral importance, for it prompts those involved to ask the question: what patterns are now operative in our lives? Second, the family would recognize that the arrival of a child affects the family as family and not just individual lives. Family members will be likely, therefore, to share information, thoughts, and feelings (coordination). Similarly the celebration of the sacrament of baptism would be seen in communal rather than individualistic terms, affecting the family as a whole and not just the child baptized. Third, in all the questions and issues that arise, the family would focus on the present situation, not allowing the process to be preempted by relapsing into patterns determined by past family history. This is pastorally significant because it means that the significance of baptism for this family will be found in the present and not in a nostalgic or thoughtless repeating of inherited ways of proceeding nor in superstitious or socially motivated attitudes towards the future.

Initial Response and Trial Solution Phase

Here likewise the family would be doing three sets of things. First, it would look to outside sources for support (configuration), instead of regarding it as a private family matter. From a pastoral perspective this translates into the process of building the broader community. Second, the family would allow and encourage all its members to provide whatever input they wished and would come to a joint course of action in which each had his or her role (coordination). In the process the family discusses plans and adjusts them as family members make their contributions. Third, the family would be willing to try new experiences and would be open to new sources of information (closure). This would mean pastorally that the family will cherish the uniqueness of the new child and hence the newness of its baptism, while at the same time being open to new understandings of baptism and the Christian life. This might mean reading the Scriptures, researching the meaning of the baptismal rites, or even proposing ways of preparing for and celebrating the rite.

Final Stage: Final Decision and Commitment

This stage, which launches the family into the ongoing life of a Christian family, also involves the three processes of configuration, coordination, and closure. Successful configuration might mean that the family would feel happy about what it had accomplished together or at least that it had learned something from its mistakes. In this way the event is remembered and celebrated for its significance, while the process is kept alive and moved forward by the memory and the commemorations. Second, the family would continue to care for one another in appropriate ways and would keep alive the spirit of mutual respect, which is represented by efforts made to achieve consensus. One example of this might be participatory reviews of family life, to see how well the baptismal commitment is being lived out. Third, the family's self-understanding would alter in some significant way. For example it might define itself in terms of an ongoing relationship to the process of initiation in the family.

What we have given here by way of examples and pastoral suggestions are merely some initial applications of the work of David Reiss and Mary Oliveri cited above, and much more could be done—and should be done—to draw out the pastoral implications of this sort of understanding of how a family works. Above all, however, it should be understood that this is a hypothetical portrait of a fully functioning family. A real family, striving to make sense of what is going on and trying to discover what to do for the best, will need support and encouragement if it is to move towards such an open style of family life and not take refuge in pseudosolidarity or relapse into laissez-faire individualism. These two latter alternatives will prove barren soil for Word and sacrament.

It may seem odd to speak of the birth of a new child as constituting a crisis in the life of a family, for few things are supposed to be as delightful and enjoyable as having a baby. In fact, however, beneath the cultural veneer of joy and congratulations which our culture requires of our public moments, at least, there are often conflicting, even negative emotions at work, which need to be recognized. Even where the child is keenly desired and gratefully welcomed, the experience of having a new child or sibling is always demanding and likely to put even the best of attitudes to the test. The point is not to debunk the myths of motherhood and family joy, but to put in a plea for realism, recognizing that the child—

even the newborn—is not the passive recipient of its elders' loving ministrations, but an active, if unconsciously active, participant in the family constellation. The child is no tabula rasa but an autonomous source of joy and anxiety, hopes and fears, demands and satisfactions, which will confront the family's sense of itself and challenge its members' self-images as well as their habitual patterns of managing life. From this perspective it can be seen that initiation is not merely something parents do for their children, but something children also do for their parents. It is not something the parish does for the family, but also something the family does for the parish. It is not necessary to wait until the child is of age before baptism can be a sacrament of conversion and commitment. Conversion and new commitments are in order from the time the child is on the way.

In such a perspective it is easy enough to understand what Rabbi Edwin Friedman means when he refers to all major ceremonies and rites of passage as processes of conversion. It is for this reason that he insists upon the need to distinguish the rite from the process:

> Perhaps the most important point to be made about distinguishing the ceremony from the passage is that the potential for change . . . could not be that great if the event were just the event.[47]

Friedman, writing from a wealth of pastoral and clinical experience, identifies some common kinds of conversion which take place in and around rites of passage: resolution of conflicts between family members, reallocation of responsibilities within a family, sharing the family story, reestablishing contact with distant relatives, getting in touch with the strongest and most formative emotional forces in one's life, recognizing typical patterns in the way a family habitually relates to the wider community and to the transcendent dimensions of life.

Friedman is speaking of rites of passage—births, deaths, marriages—in general, but his perspective certainly includes baptism. This passage is a time of transition which lasts from conception to the time when the child is fully integrated as a unique person in the life of the family. This transition time gives the family and its members the opportunity to confront their acknowledged and unacknowledged outlooks and patterns of relating. This is not easy; it is often much more convenient simply to ignore the potential for change and to treat the event as if it were just the event. Further reflection on the implications of all this for families and parishes provides a promising area of pastoral development.

Questions: How can the hidden dimensions of crisis in the birth and baptism of a child be brought to the surface?

What implications does this family systems approach have for considering the role of the sponsors or godparents in infant baptism? (The same question might be asked about the extended family, especially the grandparents of the child, whether they are still alive or not.)

What implications might this principle have for the life of the parish as such? What implications might it have for the ministerial style of the pastoral staff?

How do such practical or symbolic decisions as naming the child, deciding on a time and place for baptism, deciding who to invite, and deciding whether to ask for private or public baptism, shed light, both in the decision made and in the manner in which the decision is made, upon the way the family and/or the parish envision the meaning of initiation?

PRINCIPLE SEVEN: *The effectiveness of the initiation process depends largely upon the levels of coherence which are to be found both within the child's nuclear family and in the primary religious community (for example the parish). These levels of coherence can to some extent be empirically described.*

Empirical research has established a close association between the style of parenting adopted by parents and the personality traits of their children. While not all aspects or variables of parenting have been investigated to the same extent, two issues do seem to be pivotal: how parents share their *authority* with their children and how they share *affection*.

While we shall be using the terms authority and affection in what follows, it would be as well for the reader to understand those terms quite flexibly, perhaps reading responsibility or sense of mission for authority, for example. Interpreting authority in such a broad sense would allow us to take into account research such as that done by Dr. Jessie Potter, a sex educator.[48] Dr. Potter claims, on the basis of her decades of clinical work, that there is a relationship between how young people experience transcendent natural experiences, such as mountains or storms, and how they approach sexuality. Youths who have transcendental experiences of nature, she claims, are more likely to respect their own sexuality. This would suggest in turn that any experience of something awesome outside oneself or something impressively bigger than oneself—something which can make a claim on one—may be highly instrumental in the development of the mature individual. If Dr. Potter is right in this, this might have something important to say about the process of initiation, suggesting that it should take place in relation to something not able to be scaled down to the personal level, something which can make a claim on the loyalties of the baptized and growing child. This in turn implies that the nuclear family too is part of and recognizably loyal to a larger community. Yet this is particularly problematic today in view of the acknowledged "privatization" of both the nuclear family and religious commitment.[49]

In the 1950s and early 1960s, studies of family life concentrated particularly on measuring the extent to which parents shared power and affection with their children.[50] Since that time further research has led to the development of a fourfold typology of personality in relation to four styles of parenting. The four styles of parenting in turn are identified by measuring high and low levels of sharing in the two realms of affection and power. The following table charts children's personality traits in relation to parenting styles:

Parenting Style	Child's Personality
high shared power and high shared affection	friendly and well-adjusted
low shared power and high shared affection	conformist
low shared power and low shared affection	aggressive antisocial
high shared power and low shared affection	task-competent emotionally cold

Researchers have found strong statistical associations between the four styles of parenting indicated above and the corresponding personality traits in children. This is not, of course, predictable in any deterministic sense, but it does indicate which kinds of parenting are likely to foster which kinds of personality traits in young people. From a slightly different perspective, other researchers have shown that children who accept and get along well with their parents are more inclined to accept their parents' values.[51]

What all this comes down to is that when parents share power or responsibility with their children, they help the children become more realistic about life and more sensitive and responsive to the needs of those around them. When parents are good at sharing affection with their children and can express their love for them naturally, the children tend to be more self-accepting and find it easier to express their own love and affection for others. Families that score high on both counts, that is, those in group 1 of the chart, seem to have more coherent family lives, in the sense that the members are more likely to share the same values, to be more accepting of one another, and to be more adaptive and competent in handling the tasks of family life.

What this would seem to suggest for Christian initiation is that the success of the process will be affected by the degree to which first the family and then the local community are able to express affection and share responsibility. This in turn raises the question of whether it might not be possible—indeed necessary—to determine, on the basis of these two factors of affection and power-sharing, whether a family or a parish is ready to undertake the tasks of Christian initiation. (These are questions the parish might ask of its parish staff, its CCD program, or its school.) Translated into religious terms, power-sharing becomes responsibility for mission, shared affection becomes the life of charity, and coherence refers to what in the New Testament is called *communio* or *koinonia* and may be what is referred to today as a sense of community. In any case if the insights and vocabulary of this kind of research have any bearing upon values upheld in the Christian tradition, then they will need to be incorporated into the process of initiation which brings newcomers into that tradition. That will be done by looking at the many different dimensions of daily life and ministry which constitute the nuclear family and the parish community.

Further light on the readiness of parish and family to assume the task of initiating the young can be gleaned from anthropological studies, which have examined and compared the value systems of different cultures. A major concern of crosscultural anthropology in the 1950's was to establish appropriate criteria by which different cultures could be compared with one another. Among the pioneers in this work was Florence Kluckhohn, who identified five broad value orientations which are present in every culture, indeed every family, which would allow anthropologists to compare one culture with another, one family with another.[52] These five value orientations represent attitudes or ways of relating to human nature, activity, the relationship of human beings to their natural environment, their relationship to time, and their relationship to their fellow human beings. Different cultures live out these relationships in very different ways, each having preferred ways of doing so, tolerated ways of doing so, and unacceptable or proscribed ways of doing so. If we take middle-class Americans as an example, Kluckhohn's model reveals the following characteristic value orientations:

In relation to:	Characteristic orientations are:		
	preferred	permitted	proscribed
Human nature	evil	part good, part evil	good
Activity	doing	being	being in becoming
Nature environment	man over nature	nature over man	harmony with nature
Time	future	present	past
Relationships	individualistic	peer	hierarchical

Kluckhohn suggested that these categories of orientation might be useful for discovering "which kinds of strains are common to families and particular sub-cultures and what additional ones are to be expected when a family is in process of inculturation."[53] In other words, it is especially in times of cultural change or in cases where a family is moving from one culture or subculture to another, that these value orientations become apparent. Generally they remain pretty much unconscious and deep-rooted. In Kluckhohn's words they are "so pervasive that they markedly affect the patterns of behavior and thought of a people in all areas of activity."[54] Despite their being unconscious, however, they serve to give cultures and communities their characteristic way of being in the world— what Virginia Satir calls "meta-rules" and Eric Berne calls "scripts"— so they serve to differentiate clearly between those who are members of a family and those who are not, between those who belong to a culture and those who do not, between members of a community and outsiders. Since initiation implies inculturation, it is manifestly important that children be raised to know, if only unconsciously, the "ways of their people." In the case of adult converts, the clash of cultures involved in leaving behind one set of value orientations in order to embrace those of a Christian community will be quite stressful and will help to bring to the surface the respective values and orientations of the two systems.

This is a line of pastoral reflection which seems very promising. In view of our present concern summarized in our seventh principle, we want to bring the discussion back to the issues of power-sharing and sharing affection and to reexamine them in the light of Kluckhohn's work.

The tabulation of Kluckhohn's reading of middle-class American culture identifies fifteen possible categories of value orientation, each one of which is a manifestation of how power and love could be shared or withheld. If we look at how human beings are supposed to relate to the physical environment, for example, it is not too hard to see that where power is emphasized there will be a tendency to try to dominate the environment, whereas where power is played down the environment will seem to dominate human life. A balanced view of the uses of power and a sense of shared responsibility is likely to lead to people being ecologically sensitive and striking a balance between respect for nature and the necessary use of natural resources. Similarly with affection using the same example, an individual or a culture that is not adept at expressing affection is likely to tend toward the domination of the natural world, by extravagant consumption for example. Inability to share affection, on the other hand, can make a person overly dependent upon material possessions, while a balanced affective life would incline a person to a balanced relationship with nature and with the material world.

Every culture—whether it be the American middle class, the Hispanic American community, or a Polynesian tribe—derives its coherence from the kind of value preferences that prevail in it. The same seems to be true of families and of religious communities such as parishes. Where a Christian family or a Christian parish is concerned, the experience of initiating a new member can become the occasion for becoming more conscious of the value orientations implicit in habitual ways of acting and reacting. The categories developed by Kluckhohn could be used to explore the possibility of developing criteria for what would constitute successful initiation. What are the kinds of values by which we are now living? What kinds of values do we communicate? Nevertheless, it is important to realize that Christianity must not be identified with specific combinations of values on Kluckhohn's chart. Kluckhohn herself operated on the assumption that there was no single set of preferred value orientations that were universally normative. Hers is merely a tool for identifying and surfacing factors that are frequently lived out unconsciously by families and communities. Similarly if Christianity really is intended to be incarnated in different cultures, it cannot afford to absolutize any one cultural pattern, but it will hold them all up to the light of the Gospel.[55]

The discussion of this seventh principle, which points to the importance of coherence in the life of the family and the community, has drawn upon two separate but related strands of research. The model of sharing power and affection points to the need to reflect upon the interpersonal and intergenerational dynamics which are operative both in the child's family and in the parish community. Kluckhohn's value orientation schema encourages us to inquire into what values we actually live by, into how the Gospel may take different forms in different cultural milieux, and into the identification of contradictions between professed and realized values, or between the values of the Gospel and the values of the culture in the process of initiation. Either way a long, laborious process is involved, but the results are likely to be worth it.

Conclusion

On completing this review of insights and findings from the social sciences, it is important to remember the role of paradox or dialectic which we discussed early in this chapter. Throughout these seven principles there runs a series of tensions—tensions between individual and community, between family and society, between event and process, between past histories and present circumstances, between present realizations and future possibilities, between overachievement and underachievement, and the rest. The reminder of such tensions or dialectics is important, for they suggest something of the complexity, the unpredictability, and the uniqueness of every individual life, every family, and every community. It puts us on our guard against trying to set up a program of initiation on the basis of some supposedly "scientific" finding and expecting it to produce predictable results.

What all these findings point to is the pastoral possibility and necessity of the family's thoroughgoing involvement *both* in the process of their child's initiation *and* in the celebration of the liturgies of initiation. Of course families are usually involved anyway for better or worse. What these reflections have tried to do is indicate some of the far-reaching ways in which they are involved, but which are usually neglected in pre- and postbaptismal ministry and glossed over in the rites themselves. Examples include the parents' real—if unacknowledged—attitudes to change, especially to the change wrought in their lives by the arrival of this child. Pastoral responsibility invites family members to examine how they may unknowingly carry-over past, unproductive, and sometimes quite baneful patterns of dealing with life, especially life in the family and relationships between generations. These patterns, as well as the characteristic ways in which a given family relates to the outer world and to the larger society, are the arena of what are known in faith terms as sin and grace.

Particularly critical issues for our time are those already referred to: the privatization of the family, its restriction to the sphere of private emotional satisfaction, and its gradual exclusion from areas of life such as education, health care, and work, areas where it once was central. All this creates an additional identity crisis for the family, which even in the best of times has to juggle the tasks and live with the ambiguities described in this chapter. Reflection upon the life—and the Christian life—of the family is not a luxury for those charged with pastoral care. As this chapter has tried to show, many of the patterns of family life are to be found also in the parish. In many respects the crisis of the family is the same as the crisis of the parish. For the truth of the matter is that, as we have seen repeatedly in these pages, the parish is not merely a conglomerate of families entrusted to its pastoral care, but it is itself in many respects a family writ large. Just as the arrival and upbringing of a child challenge the resources of a family and reveal its limitations, so does Christian initiation, even for infants, reveal the hidden and unconscious dynamics of the parish itself.

Footnotes

1. Clifford Geertz, "Religion as a Cultural System," *Anthropological Approaches to the Study of Religion*, ed. Michael Banton (London: Methuen, 1968) 1–46. (Also published in C. Geertz, *The Interpretation of Culture* (New York: Basic Books, 1973).

2. For example, *Insight and Responsibility* (New York: Norton, 1964); *Toys and Reasons* (New York: Norton, 1977).

3. Jean Piaget and B. Inhelder, *The Psychology of the Child* (New York: Basic Books, 1969).

4. *Ibid.* 9–10. See also Hans G. Furth, *Piaget and Knowledge* (Englewood Cliffs, N.J.: Prentice-Hall, 1969) 46–51.

5. Lawrence Kohlberg, "Stage and Sequence: The Cognitive-Developmental Approach to Socialization," *Handbook of Socialization Theory and Research*, ed. David A. Goslin (Chicago: Rand McNally) 1969.

6. See Andrew Thompson, "Towards a Social Psychology of Religious Valuing," *Chicago Studies* 19 (1980) 3, 271–289.

7. James Youniss "Another Perspective on Social Cognition," *Minnesota Symposia on Child Psychology*, vol. 9, ed. A. D. Pick (Minneapolis: University of Minnesota Press, 1975) 173–193; "Dialectical Theory and Piaget on Social Knowledge," *Human Development* 21 (1978) 234–247; See also *Parents and Peers in Social Development* (Chicago: Chicago University Press, 1980). See also Erwin Staub, *Positive Social Behavior and Morality: Socialization and Development* (New York: Academic Press, 1979).

8. Erik Erikson, see note 2 above.

9. The best introduction to Jung's thought remains his autobiographical *Memories, Dreams, Reflections* (New York: Vintage Books, 1961). See also M. Esther Harding, *The I and the Not-I* (New York: Pantheon Books, 1965).

10. See Andrew Thompson, "Empirical Research and Religious Experience," *Aesthetic Dimensions of Religious Education*, ed. Gloria Durka (New York: Paulist, 1979) 185–201.

11. Joseph Bogen, "The Other Side of the Brain, II: An Appositional Mind," *Bulletin of the Los Angeles Neurological Societies*, 34 (1969) 3, 135–162.

12. Victor Turner, *The Ritual Process* (Chicago: Aldine, 1969).

13. But see P.-M. Gy, "La notion chrétienne d'initiation," *La Maison Dieu* 132 (1977) 33–54.

14. See note 3 above. Also Hans Furth, *Piaget and Knowledge.*

15. William McCready sums up his study by saying: "There are at least three points worth mentioning: (1) the quality of the relationship between the adults in a young person's life (is) critically important; (2) the differences between people from different ethnic heritages are great enough to make univocal policy-making unworkable; and (3) the impact of the institutional church, with the possible exception of the Catholic school, is very little, taking these other factors into account." "The Family and Socialization," *The Family in Crisis or in Transition*, Andrew Greeley (New York: Seabury Press, 1979) 33.

16. Bruno Bettelheim, *The Uses of Enchantment* (New York: Vintage Books, 1975).

17. *That They May Know You*, Andrew Thompson (Washington: National Catholic Educational Association, 1982) 74–77.

18. "Roots, Motives and Patterns in Children's Prosocial Behavior," *The Development and Maintainance of Prosocial Behaviors: International Perspectives*, ed. J. Reykowski (New York: Plenus Press, 1983). See also her articles in *Child Development* 50 (1979) 319–330; and 52 (1981) 1274–1282.

19. See, for example, Murray Bowen, "Towards the Differentiation of Self in One's Own Family," *Family Interaction: A Dialogue Between Family Researchers and Family Therapists*, ed. James Framo (New York: Springer, 1972) 111–168.

20. Sonya L. Rhodes, "A Developmental Approach to the Life-Cycle of the Family." *Social Casework* 58 (1977) 5, 301–311.

21. Talcott Parsons, "On the Concept of Value-Commitments," *Sociological Inquiry*, 38 (1968) 2, 138.

22. See *Childhood and Socialization. Recent Sociology, n. 5*, ed. H. P. Dreitzel (New York: Macmillan, 1973).

23. This example is borrowed from a videotape of Russ Ackoff, *Lecturing on Systems Theory and Principles of Management.*

24. Gerald K. Rubin, "General Systems Theory: An Organismic Conception

for Teaching Modalities of Social Work Intervention," *Smith College Studies in Social Work* 43 (1973) 206–219.

25. Ludwig von Bertanlaffy, "General Systems Theory and Psychiatry," *American Handbook of Psychiatry*, vol. 3, ed. S. Arieti (New York: Basic Books, 1966) 706–721.

26. *Ibid.* 709.

27. Ludwig von Bertanlaffy, *Organismic Psychology and Systems Theory* (Barre, Mass.: Clark University Press, 1968).

28. F. Kenneth Berrien, *General and Social Systems* (New Brunswick, N.J.: Rutgers University Press, 1968).

29. This section on the principles of systems theory draws heavily upon Steven Preister, "Systems Theory as a Framework for Family Study," *The American Family*, ed. Danuta Mostwin (Washington: Catholic University Press, 1977) 31–49.

30. Bowen, "Towards the Differentiation of Self" 117–120.

31. Herbert Anderson, *The Family and Pastoral Care* (Philadelphia: Fortress, 1984).

32. Edwin Friedman, "Systems and Ceremonies: A Family View of Rites of Passage," *The Family Life-Cycle*, ed. Elizabeth Carter and Monica McGoldrick (New York: Gardner Press, 1980) 429–460.

33. *Ibid.* 429.

34. *Ibid.* 459–460.

35. John Bossy, "The Counter-Reformation and the People of Catholic Europe," *Past and Present* 47(1970)51–70. See also Andrew Thompson, "Parish and Family: An Historic Tension," *American Catholic Family Newsletter* 1 (1982) 2, 1.10–12.

36. *Familiaris Consortio*, Apostolic Exhortation on the Family, December 15, 1981 (Washington: United States Catholic Conference) n. 70.

37. "Family Styles of Interacting," *National Institute of Mental Health Monographs: Families Today*, vol. 1 (Washington: Department of Health, Education, and Welfare, 1979) 177ff.

38. *Ibid.*

39. David Reiss, "The Family's Construction of Social Reality and Its Ties to Its Kin Network: An Exploration of Casual Direction," *Journal of Marriage and the Family* 43 (1981) 391–407. See also *The Family's Construction of Reality* (Cambridge: Harvard University Press, 1981).

40. T. W. Adorno, et al, *The Authoritarian Personality* (New York: Harper, 1950).

41. Milton Rokeach, *The Open and Closed Mind* (New York: Basic Books, 1960).

42. Milton Rokeach, *Beliefs, Attitudes and Values* (Palo Alto, Calif.: Jossey-Bass, 1968).

43. This threefold description of trust is quite consistent with Erik Erikson's work on the same topic. See *Insight and Responsibility*; "The Development of Ritualization," *The Religious Situation: 1968*, ed. Donald Cutler (Boston: Beacon Press, 1968); and *Toys and Reasons*.

44. John Dewey, *How Do We Think?* (New York: D. C. Heath, 1910). See also, Sidney Simon, *Values in Education* (Columbus: Merrill, 1966).

45. James Aldous, "A Framework for the Analysis of Family Problem-Sharing," *Family Problem-Solving*, ed. James Aldous, et al. (Hinsdale, Ill.: Dryden, 1971).

46. David Reiss and Mary E. Oliveri, "Family Paradigm and Family Coping," *Family Relations* 29 (1980) 431–444.

47. Friedman, "Systems and Ceremonies" 436.

48. J. Potter, "Masculine, Feminine or Human," Tape #C-5238, National Catholic Reporter Cassettes (Kansas City, Mo., 1980).

49. See Herbert Anderson, "The Family Under Stress: A Crisis of Purpose," *Moral Issues and Christian Response*, 3rd ed., ed. Paul T. Jersild (New York: Holt, Rinehart and Winston, 1983) 114–124.

50. See Murray Strauss, "Power and Support Structure of the Family in Relation to Socialization," *Journal of Marriage and the Family* 27(1964) 318–326.

51. See Merton Strommen, *A Study of Generations* (Minneapolis: Augsburg, 1973) and *Five Cries of Youth* (New York: Harper and Row, 1974). See also Andrew D. Thompson, "The Central Role of Family in Youth's Religious Socialization," *That They May Know You*, Andrew Thompson (Washington: National Catholic Educational Association, 1982) 74–77.

52. Florence Kluckhohn, "Variations in the Basic Values of Family Systems," *A Modern Introduction to the Family*, ed. Norma W. Bell (New York: Free Press, 1968) 319–330. See also *Social Casework* 39 (1958) 63–72.

53. *Ibid.* 319.

54. *Ibid.* 319.

55. Andrew D. Thompson, "Towards a Social-Psychology of Religious Valuing," *Chicago Studies* 19 (1980) 3, 271–289.

3. PASTORAL CARE IN THE PROCESS OF INITIATION

Herbert Anderson

Initiation and Paradox

The arrival of a child into the worlds of family and Church is both a gift and a challenge. It is a gift of new life because the unpredictable but creative energies of the newly born invigorate human community, even though the task of caring for the young is an exhausting one. The arrival of a child is a gift of hope that reaffirms our belief in the future that God continues to make new. It is a gift of love because the spontaneous affection of an infant reminds us over and over again that transcending love is never conditional. Our affirmation that children are a gift is ultimately grounded in the conviction that the birth of a child is a gift of God's self for the sake of creation and a sign of God's providence.

The addition of a child is also a challenge to our reluctance to change because it requires that the family and other communities modify previously determined and sometimes fixed patterns of interaction. It is a challenge to our inclinations toward selfishness and short-range thinking because an infant always calls us out of ourselves into ever-widening environments. The arrival of a child is a challenge to our search for safety in sameness because each child is a new creation of God with unique gifts to give to the world. The birth of a child is a sign that the world is a constantly changing creation of God.

The process by which an infant is incorporated into a family and other communal contexts is a delicate balance between the needs of the individual and the needs of the community. In the previous chapter we have identified seven principles from the human sciences that inform our understanding of the paradoxical nature of human development from the beginning of life. Each of these principles is governed by the conviction that all initiation is marked by paradox. From the beginning of life, the rituals and ceremonies that shape our entrance into and our existence in community also modulate the balance between the needs of the individual and the demands of the sustaining environments.

This ritual mediation between the poles of a paradox is, in the instance of birth and baptism, a mediating between whole-hearted participation in community and whole-hearted support of the growth of individuals. The event/process of baptism is in the interest of maintaining a balance between the needs of the individual and the needs of the community. For parents the birth of a child is an act of faith in the future that God is making new. For the Christian community it is a sign that the story of God will be remembered for yet another generation. And yet the child and the child's future with God in the Church and in the world must be the central focus from the beginning. The rituals of birth and the event/process of baptism mediate this fundamental paradox of the individual in community.

Because of the importance and complexity of the birth of a child for all human communities, it is understandable that the Christian Church has maintained a sacrament of initiation in infancy that both incorporates and individuates. Baptism makes an individual a particular child of God and locates him or her in the midst of an assembly of Christians. Baptism is the sacrament that particularizes each individual as a unique gift of God at the same time that it incorporates each one into the mystical Body of Christ, blurring individuality for the sake of the whole. Baptism supports the process of individuation by which we come to be distinct and autonomous selves while recognizing the necessity for community in human life.

As a ritual of initiation, baptism is both an event and a process. It is a momentary and complete action that begins a lifelong struggle for human renewal that is punctuated by subsequent sacraments of the Church. Nothing needs to be added to what is accomplished in the ritual of baptizing, and yet that event cannot be isolated from the process that succeeds from it. The rites of baptism constitute the child in a new set of relationships in the Church within which the child is nourished in the faith for a life of responsible discipleship.

The relationship between the family into which one is born or adopted and the Christian community into which one is baptized is a reciprocal one. On the one hand the process of parenting is enhanced by the awareness that the children in our homes belong to God. The second birth of baptism initiates each individual into an assembly in which the Christian story is remembered and from which each individual is drawn beyond the family into larger and larger communities of concern. On the other hand Christian discipleship requires men and women who have been raised in families in which individual gifts are discovered and fostered. Parents are to protect and nurture their children so that they might become autonomous enough for service in the world on behalf of Christ. For that reason the task of welcoming and nourishing the newly arrived is a profoundly religious responsibility for the family. From the beginning of life, parents are to honor unique gifts of each child for the sake of Christian discipleship.

The family and the Church are not only reciprocal contexts promoting human growth and development, they are also communities in which the ambiguities of life are visible. Rites of initiation take up and define the transcendent meaning of birth and growth, but they also highlight the ways in which we impede the movement toward autonomy and hence restrict the full possibilities of Christian discipleship. Even when we can hide our sinfulness in the Church, it is almost impossible to cover over our frailties in the family. Relationships are blurred, ill-defined, and ambiguous enough that growth toward maturity is impaired. Because the rites of birth and rebirth put into sharp focus both the light and dark sides of our lives and relationships, we need to be reminded that assemblies of Christians are always forgiving communities.

The connections between the rituals of birth into a family and the ritual of rebirth into Christ's Body are significant but have not always been made explicit. The intent of this series about alternative futures for worship is to revitalize the ritual moment by connecting the Church's rites with the vital experiences of individual and corporate life. The rites and sacraments of the Church are symbols of God's living presence throughout all of life. All of nature and history reflect the graciousness of God to which particular sacraments bear witness. This study will examine the rites of initiation by which the newly arrived are particularized and incorporated into the family and the Church for growth toward discipleship.

A ritual is a sacred moment in a series of many moments that provides a framework for processes of human transformation. Faith and identity have their beginnings in ordinary experiences in infancy through which we come eventually to be hopeful about the future and responsive to the possibility that God will indeed make something new. Through the rituals of welcoming, naming, feeding, and elimination the child develops a sense of the numinous in life. "This is the very ground for higher forms of rituals of religious faith in which human beings feel in the living presence of God and 'see' the meaning of life in the 'face' of God as the child sees the light of the parent's love and affirmation in the luminous eyes and smiling face of the parent."[1] The rites themselves do not guarantee attitudes of the heart that enhance creative transformation, nor do we do this work alone. Religious rituals of initiation express and celebrate God's work among us in making all things new.

There are three foci for the many moments in the process by which the newly arrived become a part of those relational webs that will nurture them toward the fullness of humanity. The first task is to create a welcoming environment. This process begins long before the child is born and continues long after the birth. Gestation is itself a time of anticipation and preparation during which the family seeks to create a hospitable context that has both time and space for the arrival of an infant. An environment is hospitable when there is both space and time for nurture.

The second task is to create a holding environment. Each child is unique. That uniqueness is the gift of something new that reflects God's ongoing creative work in the world. From the beginning (which may be even before the child is born) we attend to the particular needs and gifts of each child in order to foster individuality. The bonding between parents and children that inevitably results from that attending will be appropriate whenever it is more devoted to the needs of the child than those of the parent. We hold our children gently so that it is easy to let them go. Baptism is a constant reminder to parents, from the beginning of a new life, that the child in their midst is theirs and not theirs. It brings into sharp focus our human impulse to hold onto our children in ways that inhibit their movement toward autonomy.

Finally the birth of a child is an act of faith on the part of parents that also requires faithfulness. Both birth and baptism presuppose a believing environment. For Christian parents baptism is a sign that human life is sustained by the One who keeps promises. Although it is essential that parents fulfill their nurturing responsibilities toward their children, God's trustworthiness ultimately transcends their own efforts to be a dependable "hallowed presence." Trust, hope, and love are born in a child through the reciprocity of parental care and God's dependability. Because God keeps promises, parents are free to care for their children without being overly protective or anxious.

Making a Welcoming Environment

Hospitality is one of the marks of the Christian life. Showing hospitality is a metaphor for the Gospel. It is the willingness to attend to the stranger in our midst. It is an active reaching out to welcome the stranger, so he or she finds a place to belong. The stranger is not just someone unknown or a foreigner or the beggar at the gate; it is anyone outside our skin. In this sense the children who come to live with us are strangers whom we welcome. To show hospitality to our children is to welcome them as individuals with gifts to give that will enrich the family's life. In the beginning the newly arrived child whom we want to welcome hospitably may appear to take more than he or she gives. If, however, we are looking for ways to receive the gifts that our children have to give from the beginning, we will find them in abundance.

The signs of a hospitable environment are deceptively simple. It is a context in which affection is shown without binding the recipient and where there is freedom without abandonment. It is a physical and emotional space in which there is room to grow, to become ourselves, and where we are regarded from the beginning as individuals of worth, whose being will enhance the whole. It is a free space in the sense that the expectations are explicit and the affection is unconditional. An environment that is hospitable has clear boundaries that can nonetheless be modified. If the boundaries are too porous, it is no longer a free space. If on the other hand the invisible separations or boundaries are too rigid, they become like walls that prevent access of members to one another and thereby promote premature abandonment.

The addition of a child to a family is a challenge to its capacity to be hospitable. It calls for the willingness and ability to welcome a child into an environment that has both space and time to attend to the nurturing needs of the newly born. The arrival of a child demands that the family modify its space so there is room enough to grow without fear of abandonment. The story that a friend of mine has told about his birth describes an environment made up of several adults who were eager to welcome a child into their midst. It was a welcoming space, but it was not free because there were spoken expectations that established certain conditions on his becoming.

How many of them were there in the house on that cold June day? All of them gone now, all those people whose lives are to be celebrated here. When the story is told, it is told as though they were all present; but the grandfathers, J. O. and Bert, were somehow the actors. They paced the living room of that house, the glassblower and the carpenter, helpless craftsmen. They shivered, I'm told, with the unusual chill of that late spring, until one proposed to the other that they build a fire.

It was the day for the baby to be born. Due in mid-May, the baby had delayed until now. But it was to be so, they said. On the day before Louise had taken a big dose of castor oil to start the labor process. Now in the small hours of the morning, she was at work. Today must be the day. It was Minnie's birthday, and her son Ernest's too. So of course the baby would be born to celebrate Ernest's thirty-third and his mother's fifty-fifth. The baby owed it to them. He—it would be a boy; no girls' names had been considered—would surely arrive now. And he did. His world was gathered to welcome him, to tell him who he was to be, to predict, to adore, to demand, to celebrate, to love, to define.

There is little doubt that this child was welcomed by a family that had long awaited his coming. From before he was born, this child had a special place in that family. There was room enough, despite the great company of adults who shared the same space. However, there were obligations embedded in the family's anticipations. It was not insignificant for this child's life that he was born on the birthday of his father and fraternal grandmother. He would mark out the years of his life according to already established dates. He would eventually know the strings that were attached to his welcome, but they were already at work from the beginning.

When there are children in the family already, they participate in the preparations for welcoming the child with mixture of delight and jealousy. I am told that I was not hospitable about the birth of my brother after four and a half years of ruling the roost. I made it perfectly clear that he was an unwelcome addition to *my* house. Handling the ambivalence of children about the birth of a sibling is an important part of creating a hospitable environment. Sometimes the expectations for a new sibling are positive and quite specific with regard to gender or talent. The following true story is a delightful account of childhood magic. Orders for brothers or sisters are seldom filled as directly or as promptly as this one was.

One morning my mother and I, along with an older brother, sat down with a Montgomery Ward catalog before us. I was nine years old at the time. Neither my brother nor I knew that our mother was pregnant. In those years women wore loose-fitting garments. My mother asked whether my brother and I would like to have a new baby in the house. We thought it was a grand idea. We selected a baby from the baby pages in the catalog and my mother promised to place the order. The delivery was less than three months later. Since the baby was to be born at home, we were all conveniently shuttled off with friends on the day of the birth. When we returned the next morning, there was the baby. We thought the order had been filled very well. It was a boy.

Everyone in a family needs to be involved in creating a hospitable environment for the addition of a child. When the expectations of children are very concrete, disappointment may temporarily sour a welcome. On other occasions children unambiguously participate in the celebrations marking the arrival of a new family member. Most children are aware that the stork does not bring babies nor can one order them from the Montgomery Ward catalog. Being present at the birth is one appropriate and nonmagical way of involving children in the arrival of a new sibling. One eleven-year-old who was present at the birth called a friend immediately to announce that "we just had a baby." Parents should be encouraged to do whatever they can do to include their children in making a hospitable space for the arrival of another child.

It is not always easy to create an appropriately hospitable space for the addition of a child. Sometimes all available family space is already filled by the needs of other children, parental relationships, professional responsibilities, or other activities. The inability to create a welcoming space may also be the result of the limited emotional resources of parents who are unable to respond to the demands of the newly born.

Sometimes the birth of a child is expected to fill an empty space in the lives of parents. That empty space may have resulted from the death of a parent or from the loss of employment outside the home by choice or by failure. The empty space may in fact be in one of the parents because of the absence of necessary parental affection. The arrival of a child is expected to fill up this emptiness. Some couples hope that the birth of a child will save a troubled marriage by making a bridge between the marital pair. When the child is expected to fill up an emptiness it cannot possibly fill, the parent's disappointment may lead to serious consequences. That is how it was for José and Marie.

Marie had decided shortly after she and José Garcia were married that she would give up her position at the bank in order to be at home. She very much wanted to create a different home environment than she had known as a child. She worked very hard during the first year of their marriage to add "homey" touches to their modest apartment. Marie was ecstatic when she discovered that she was pregnant. So was José. During most of her pregnancy, José worked overtime in order to put aside some extra money for the baby. Working extra hours was easier for José than knowing how to respond to the radical emotional shifts that Marie experienced during pregnancy. As a result José found reasons to spend less and less time at home. The more José was away, the more Marie wanted the baby all to herself. When the baby was born, José felt more and more excluded and found all kinds of excuses to stay away. The more he stayed away, the more Marie clung to her little girl for friendship and solace. When the child was two, she was physically abused by her mother.

When the space into which a child is born is a vacuum, the child is almost always a victim. Sometimes the damage is done by emotional bonding between a parent and a child that blurs the generational boundaries. The parent expects exclusivity and demands an inappropriate response from the child. For Marie and her daughter the conflict began when the child sought to establish her autonomy. Attending to the newly born can never be more for the sake of the parent than for the sake of the child. It is the child who suffers if he or she is expected to fill a vacuum.

Hospitality is an obligation for parents. In that sense it is like the law of the desert in the Old Testament that necessitated hospitality for the wayfarer in a hostile land. It was a matter of survival. Parents are to provide a safe place in which children are protected, nourished, and nurtured for the sake of survival and growth. Hospitality to children is also proclaimed by the Gospel. It is a sign of a providential God who looks after the vulnerable ones. Parents who provide a hospitable environment for children bear witness to God's gracious acceptance of humankind. When they can be hospitable, parents will be surprised in wonderful ways by the gifts their children have to give.

Obstacles to Welcoming the Child

Creating a hospitable environment for a child is never an easy task. There are numerous ordinary and extraordinary obstacles to work through in a family's preparation for a child's arrival. If it is the first child, there are significant adjustments that need to be made in the emotional availability and daily interaction of the marital pair. Work patterns must be altered. Even if one parent is primarily at home, the other parent needs to modify her or his work life in order to provide support and assistance in the parenting tasks. The addition of the first child, particularly, changes relationships between parents and their own fathers and mothers.

Making an emotional space for children is the hardest and most important task in becoming and being parents. It requires changes in expectations about marital interactions and emotional availability. Routines change. A couple's freedom to go to a movie or go shopping on the spur of the moment is diminished for quite some time. The kinds of changes that people need to make in order to welcome the new arrival inevitably involve loss.

Chester and Stephanie had been married for seven years before they became parents of twins. The period of pregnancy had been a difficult time of adjustment for both of them. Stephanie quit smoking, and because she gained too much weight, she had to restrict her eating as well. Chester continued eating and smoking, but it felt to him like he was more and more isolated from Stephanie. Before the pregnancy they had been an active, high energy couple who were out at least three nights a week. It was not easy for either of them to slow down. Both Chester and Stephanie were delighted to have twins, but the adjustments after the birth were even more difficult than they anticipated. Chester came to resent the twins because Stephanie could not be as available to him as before.

Even when we have taken care to prepare for the addition of children to a family, the changes are often the occasion for grief. Chester knew that the twins took just about all the emotional energy that Stephanie had. He also knew that the demands of the twins were temporary. It still took him the better part of a year to adjust to the new family situation. We need to be attentive to the ambivalent feelings of new parents. For people who are generally less tied down by their work, the addition of children is sometimes the primary experience of limitation to freedom. As friends and pastoral persons, we need to provide an accepting context for new parents to give voice to the loss of freedom and mobility that children bring to a family. The opportunity to grieve is likely to make it easier for parents to create a hospitable environment.

Parents and parents-to-be are often forced to decide between competing social values. Although we would like to believe that we can have it all, the addition of children changes a family and demands accommodation and even sacrifice. We are reluctant to give up one value for another. We would like to think we could have children without altering our life in any significant way. It is not so. The decisions are made more difficult because the values associated with being parents are not easily compatible with an achievement-oriented society that measures human worth in terms of production, possession, and consumption. By contrast, parenting often requires sacrifice, a willingness to set aside personal gain, cooperation over competitive values, and the conservation of personal energy in order to attend to the newly born.

Skip and Carla had been in graduate school since they were married. Although they had agreed when they married that they wanted children, neither was willing to set aside academic and career pursuits in order to have children. Carla's unplanned pregnancy created considerable tension in the marriage. Moreover Carla's mother, who was delighted to be a grandmother for the first time, was insisting that they move in with her, so there would be an adequate environment for the child. Skip and Carla were unanimous in their opposition to her well-intended overture. However, they could not agree on how to change their life patterns in order to make room for a child. That decision was further complicated by the fact that both Skip and Carla understood their academic careers as an expression of Christian mission. By the time they sought pastoral counsel at the Newman Center where they worshipped, their conflicts were impeding the development of a hospitable space for the yet unborn child.

There are many ways to serve God, and being a Christian parent is one of them. However, the Christian vocation of parenting is not always easy to sustain in relation to other obligations. Skip and Carla finally agreed that they should both slow down their academic programs so they would have time and emotional energy for their child, their graduate work, and each other. Helping parents-to-be make necessary accommodations in order to provide time and space for children is an exercise in facing finitude. We cannot do it all. Responsible parenting is enhanced by understanding that freedom is always finite.

Preparations for the addition of a child are sometimes seriously complicated if the prospective parents have not satisfactorily differentiated themselves from their families of origin. The interventions of well-meaning grandparents—always in the interest of the child—undercut the new parents' fragile sense of competence. Differing approaches to parenting may force husbands and wives to make choices for each other that violate presuppositions about loyalty to their families of origin.

Cliff and Rosinda had only been married for a short time before their first child was born. There had been some conflict between the families about the marriage itself and about where the couple chose to live. Both grandmothers were determined to have equal access to their first grandchild. Cliff's mother was a fastidious homemaker who kept her modern fourth floor apartment spotlessly clean. It had been that way, Cliff remembered, even when they were poor. Rosinda's upbringing had been more casual. Most of the time Rosinda's mother kept her children in diapers but not much more. The climate was warm enough for the child to be adequately clothed in only a diaper. Rosinda's mother held the conviction (somewhat fiercely) that clothes are a necessary evil because they are more for pretense than protection.

Cliff's mother showered the new child with clothes she had been sewing for several months. She was particularly proud that she had found an androgynous pattern book for baby clothes. Rosinda did not use all of the clothes. About one month after their child was born and after three visits from Cliff's mother, Cliff and Rosinda had an intense fight that was mostly about loyalty to family traditions. Cliff had in fact resented his mother's fussiness when he was a child, but in the heat of battle he defended his mother's position regarding clothes. It took Cliff and Rosinda several fights and some skillful pastoral interventions before they could admit that they both wanted to establish patterns of childrearing that were their own.

The birth of a child is a test of family loyalty that is not uncommon early in a marriage. Because grandparents are often geographically removed from their grandchildren, insisting on family traditions of childrearing may be a way of ensuring quality care from a distance. Unfortunately well-meant and unsolicited advice about infant care may be interpreted by new parents as oblique criticism. The best way that grandparents can love their grandchildren is to support the parenting of their sons and daughters. Sons and daughters who are able to leave home in order to form a marital bond are likely to be able to form a hospitable environment.

Birth and Grief

There are times when the family is fully prepared to welcome a child into its midst but that arrival is aborted by miscarriage. The termination of a pregnancy produces an uncommon grief. It is grieving for the loss of what might have been more than the loss of something we have known and held. Because of the complexity of its grief, miscarriage is a loss that leaves an indelible scar on a family.

Janet and Peter had been married for two years when they discovered that Janet was pregnant. What seemed to be stomach cramps from too much pizza was a miscarriage at three months. Janet grieved immediately. Peter was able to cry when he had to tell his parents that they would not be grandparents. The pain of this loss turned to resentment when Peter learned that his sister and her husband were expecting a baby. It seemed unfair that someone else in the family was able to have a child. By the time that his niece was born, Peter was over his resentment but much more aware of his sadness. The birth of his sister's baby made him realize how much he wanted to have children. About one year after the miscarriage, Janet thought she was pregnant again. This time they were more cautious. The home pregnancy test was positive, but the subsequent physician's test proved negative. Even though there was no miscarriage, the pain was just as intense. They told no one. For several weeks Janet would not leave the house. She was convinced that something was terribly wrong with her body. Janet's shame was deep and secret.

Miscarriage is a difficult loss to grieve. It is a loss of what might have been. For the woman it is also a loss of confidence in her body. There is a sense of shame because her body has failed. That shame is often the reason why a miscarriage becomes a family secret with buried, unresolved grief. It is very important that we be alert in ministry to the lingering grief for an aborted pregnancy. Similarly when a woman has carried a child for nine months and the family has awaited its arrival with an appropriate mixture of excitement and apprehension, the sadness and rage are almost inconsolable if it is a stillbirth.

Richard and Elaine had two daughters aged seven and five when Elaine became pregnant for a third time. Everyone in the family hoped for a little boy. As a matter of fact, only male names were considered. The girls were certain that they would have a baby brother to take care of. Richard built a bed that was sturdy enough to hold a professional football tackle. Although Elaine had been uncomfortable during this pregnancy, there was no sign of difficulty until ten days before the child was born dead. The grief of that loss was intensified by the fact that it had been a male child. Richard refused to attend the memorial Mass. He forbade talk of the death in the family and buried his grief with endless hours at work. The grieving of Elaine and her daughters was seriously compromised by Richard's sullen denial. Richard and Elaine were divorced two years after the stillbirth.

The experiences of Janet and Peter and Richard and Elaine remind us of the fragility of life from its inception. Even the warm safety of a mother's womb is not enough to fend off life-threatening forces. We are reminded in a more general way that not every birth is the occasion for joy. Even if the child lives, there may be severe physical or mental limitations that temper the parent's joy with sadness. Dreams and expectations are shattered. In such circumstances parents need freedom to grieve the loss of the child that might have been so they can eventually accept the child that is born. They may also need help from friends to have time to grieve. The demands of caring for a handicapped child may cause people to overlook the necessity of grieving. Parents and children alike need special care when the loss at birth is unexpected and difficult to express.

Sometimes the grief at birth is less understandable but equally intense. The child's gender may not fulfill the expectations of one or both parents. Some newly born are rejected outright for not being the expected gender. For others the rejection may take a more subtle form by responding to a child as though it were the desired gender. Children who are born after parents thought they were through with parenting may be received with delight or they may be regarded as a mistake or accident. Those who care for the families of the newlyborn need to pay attention to the ways in which unfulfilled expectations can negatively affect the responses of parents.

Baptism and Birth

Baptism has special significance for the unwelcome child. It has special significance when the circumstances prior to or surrounding the birth diminish the family's ability or willingness to be hospitable. A family in grief may have neither the emotional energy nor the inclination to welcome the occasion of that grief. The child who does not measure up to expectations prior to birth may never fit in the family or may only fit by violating his or her own unique gifts in order to fulfill the family's expectations. For such children it is difficult to overcome the belief that existence is almost always conditional. Baptism for those children can be a liberating event. The unwelcome child is born into a new community where belonging is never conditional because it is sealed by the promises of God.

In the best of all worlds, the family is first of all a welcoming environment that receives the newly born. It is a place of hospitality in which there is both appropriate space and necessary time to attend to the child. Hospitality is first of all an attitude that bends the family toward the needs of the newly born. That attitude of hospitality is embodied in ritual occasions through which the child is welcomed into the extended family, the neighborhood, networks of friends, and the assembly of believing Christians.

Gail Ramshaw-Schmidt's contribution to this volume offers a series of rites calculated to foster a sense of hospitality both in the family and in the local church. Even before birth the prayer of the family and friends of the coming child creates a psychological and spiritual space for the one who is to come and who is already, in a very real sense, present. Such prayer can help parents face and deal with whatever ambivalent feelings attend the prospect of the arrival of the new baby and encourage them to face the event and all that it means to them as Christians. Furthermore the local community is put on notice and thus prepared to offer the newcomer hospitality, by the rite of baptismal intent.

The postnatal rites offer the opportunity to the family and to the community to acknowledge the presence of the child, to express their joy over a successful delivery, or their pain when the child is born deformed, its life is in danger, or the child dies. Whatever the case, blessing is returned to God, for the Lord gives and the Lord takes away. Similarly after baptism the commemoration of the child's baptism at home and in church not only serves to help the child grow in its baptismal identity, but also to rehearse both the family and the parish in those attitudes of hospitality which they both pledged at baptism.

As these rites show, the child who is baptized is not only twice born, but twice welcomed. In baptism an individual is welcomed into a community which transcends the limitations of one's birth or adoptive family. However much the child's family may fail to be an adequately welcoming environment, the child can still claim a home in Christ's Church. The local congregation, gathered in the name of Jesus, is a place of hospitality by right, and baptism is the means whereby that community welcomes new members. Beginning with the reception, the actions of baptism welcome the child into the Church and incorporate him or her into a lifelong pilgrimage, a pilgrimage into the mystery of Christ's death and resurrection undertaken in the company of the rest of the baptized. Even when in later life the baptized may wonder how welcome they are in their own families of origin, they can remember the fact of their baptism and know themselves to have been welcomed into the world God has redeemed.

Providing a Holding Environment for Growth

Procreation includes more than giving birth. It is about rearing children as well as having children. Because the human animal is vulnerable and dependent for a long time at the beginning of life, it is necessary that the family—or something like it—provide a safe space to protect and nurture the young. Having and rearing children transcends cultural and historical particularities. The family participates in the continuing creative activity of God by providing for the nurture of children.

In order to provide for the nurture of children, the family needs to be a holding environment as well as a place of hospitality. From the beginning of life, children need to be held but not so tightly that neither parent nor child can let go. Because children are vulnerable, they need to be protected from possible harm without being prohibited from exploring the possibilites of their world. Because children are dependent, they need the warmth of intimacy and care without being smothered by excessive affection or closeness. Because most of all, children are human beings, they need what all people need: a hospitable place to belong to that provides them room to grow.

Tim was the first grandchild to visit the Thompsons. When he was sixteen months old, he and his parents came to visit grandma and grandpa Thompson for a long weekend. Before the young family arrived, the new grandparents scoured the house looking for things that might hurt Tim or that Tim might hurt. Small breakable items came off the coffee table in the family room; three large potted plants went upstairs; antiques came off the lowest shelf of a baker's rack; several electric light sockets were covered with plastic covers. In preparation for having an active, energetic, inquisitive sixteen-month-old child in the house for four days, the Thompsons made a number of changes in the way their house was arranged and organized. They were determined to create an environment that was both hospitable and safe; they wanted Tim to have freedom to explore without danger.

What the Thompsons experienced is by no means unfamiliar to many grandparents. Nor is it the only option. They could have done nothing to prepare for the child's arrival and then spent the weekend warning the child of danger or cautioning the child not to touch. The child is given a restricting message: be careful around grandma and her things. Other grandparents may not make any changes to prepare for the arrival of a grandchild because accidents happen. When that happens, appropriate care is extended to the child, but there is no particular effort to prevent accidents. Although it is inconvenient for grandparents to rearrange the furniture occasionally in order to entertain their grandchildren, it is even more demanding for parents to provide on an ongoing basis both a secure base from which children might explore and the freedom to do that exploring. A balance between freedom and safety is one of the chief characteristics of a hospitable holding environment.

This balance between freedom and safety is only one of the many dialectics that determine the contours of the family as a holding environment. The close physical intimacy between mother and child before birth is replaced by a psychosocial closeness that ensures the emotional warmth necessary for early development. From the beginning, however, those emotional bonds need to be balanced by a respect for the newly born as a separate and uniquely individual creation of God. Some parents establish a bond with their children in the first months that is difficult to sever when it is time for sons and daughters to leave home. The emotional bondage that results from children and parents holding on too tightly can seriously impede the development of individual autonomy. Other parents may hold a child only when necessary and in ways that lack warmth. Children from families in which nurture is without affection long to be held in order to make up for this lack in early infancy. They may also fear intimacy of any kind because it is unfamiliar. In order to create the kind of holding environment in which children are free to discover whom they might best become, the family needs to maintain a delicate balance between holding and letting go.

Richard and Jennifer had two children, a boy of ten and a boy of eight, when Jennifer became pregnant again. Because they had married later in life, Jennifer was forty-one when she was pregnant for the third time. Both parents were particularly delighted with the pregnancy when they learned that they would have a girl. Because she was determined not to risk losing her chance for a daughter, Jennifer stayed in bed for most of the pregnancy. Richard and the boys developed a deeper bond because they had to manage to do things by themselves. After Carla was born, Jennifer continued to devote her life to her daughter. She hardly let Carla out of her sight. Jennifer nursed her daughter until Carla was almost three. Because Jennifer did not trust anyone else to care for Carla, she and Richard had a limited social life. Richard was not critical of Jennifer's attachment to her daughter, but he did finally seek the counsel of a very good friend in the parish because he feared that the bond between Jennifer and Carla was affecting their marriage. In subsequent conversations with a pastoral counselor about the marriage, Jennifer was helped to see that her overcloseness with Carla could very likely be detrimental to her daughter in later life.

Jennifer's profound love for her little daughter motivated her to see how crucial it was for Carla to have some space of her own from the beginning. Because it masks itself as love, the dangers of parental overinvolvement with their children are often not discovered until it is too late. We are usually more aware of alarming situations in which children are abandoned or poorly fed and clothed because the family's limited resources are being used for drugs and alcohol. While we are appalled by such obvious instances of parental neglect, we tend to overlook other ways in which parents ignore or disregard or are unable to respond to the nurturing needs of the child. The experience of neglect lingers into adulthood. There are some adult sons and daughters who continue to think about themselves as orphans because of the emotional abandonment they experienced from the beginning of life.

It is seldom easy but always essential for families to maintain this balance between holding and letting go. Children are most likely to discover that the world and God are trustable in a holding environment that is at the same time hospitable. Children learn to mistrust early, when their needs are not met or their being is violated. Children learn how to live defensively in order to protect themselves from disappointment and hurt. Children learn that intimacy is dangerous if they are smothered by affection. A holding environment that carries its members gently and lovingly, with freedom to explore and fail within protected limits, fosters trust in the child that the world is trustworthy.

The Church is also a holding environment that cradles the faithful in their struggle for renewal. If the Church is to be a holding environment that neither promotes unnecessary dependency nor disavows the ongoing and genuine human needs for community, it will hold its members gently. Neither family nor Church are ends in themselves. They exist in order to nurture us, heal us, and help us grow to be autonomous enough to serve the world for Christ's sake. The family and the Church are holding environments that prepare us for service.

BAPTISM AND NURTURE

Becoming a separate person capable of being in community with others is a lifelong process. It begins with the physical severing of the umbilical cord that sustained the unborn child. The process continues when the child begins to move away from the emotional womb that has been nurturing and protecting it from birth. This psychological birth is enhanced by a family context in which individual uniqueness is honored from the beginning, and individual thoughts, feelings, wishes, and fantasies are validated. The kind of holding environment that parents create will significantly influence the process of individuation by which a self is formed.

The bonding that occurs in the family forms the basis for subsequent attachments in life. We are communal beings from the beginning. At the same time we are individual and distinct creations of God. The shaping of human particularity has its beginnings in the context of the family because it is not possible to be or become an individual except in relation to community. The family is a hospitable community that honors individuality. In order to provide a holding environment that fosters individuation, the family must insist paradoxically on the primacy of both the community and the individual. Personhood presupposes community; identity precedes belonging.

Before a child is born, it is the mother who provides the nutrients and environment necessary for the development of new life. This biological connection that is necessary for the survival of the fetus prior to birth continues in social forms after birth. The infant depends on nurturing ones for food and protection and mobility and warmth. W. H. Auden has a graphic picture of this utter dependency in his poem *Mundus et Infans:*

> Kicking his mother until she let go of his soul
> Has given him a healthy appetite: clearly, her role
>   In the New Order must be
> To supply and deliver his raw materials free;
>   Should there be any shortage,
> She will be held responsible; she also promises
> To show him all such attentions as befit his age.[2]

The physical and emotional well-being of the newly born depends on the ability of the nurturing ones to "deliver raw materials free" and show "all such attentions" as are needed. It is the responsibility of the parents to create the kind of holding environment in which the resources necessary for growth are available without obligation.

The bonding between parents and children that ensures the development of individual uniqueness grows out of the experience of empathy. Within the context of the family, empathy creates a holding environment in which there is freedom and safety to venture forth and make new discoveries. For parents and infants, empathy is one-directional. It is the task of the parents to attend to the needs of the newly born from the infant's perspective, without expecting to be understood in return. This empathic posture is as indispensable as oxygen for the growth of the newly born. Empathy involves the willingness and ability of parents to experience the world through the eyes of the child. This capacity for empathy transforms the family into a hospitable context in which there is support for each member's journey. When empathy is present in a family, it is likely that the child will receive "all such attentions as befit his [her] age."

Not all parents are prepared to be empathic with infants or prepared for the awesome responsibility of nurturing and protecting the newly born. Biological closeness does not guarantee emotional bonding, nor does biological parenthood automatically eventuate in adequate nurturing. Ordinarily the ability to parent grows out of the experience of being parented and whatever instincts to care are available to us. Increasing numbers of children are being born into inhospitable environments or to parents who are ill-equipped for the process. The rise of teenage pregnancies is only one illustration of this trend.

Carry was fifteen when she became a mother. She remained at home with her parents and continued to attend school after the baby was born. Teenage posters had been taken down from her walls in order to make her bedroom into a nursery. She needed to grow up in a hurry, but she could not grow up fast enough to be the kind of mother her baby needed. She wanted to go to rock concerts with her friends, but she had to stay home instead and feed her baby. It is not easy to stay being a child when you have one of your own. Having a baby to care for was more work than she wanted and more responsibility than she could handle.

The young are not the only people ill-prepared for parenting. The increase in reported incidents of child neglect and child abuse is a frightening indication that our capacity to love our children has been diminished. Our love for our children is also compromised by the expectations of personal self-fulfillment and corroded by stress from a competitive, achievement-oriented society. Our indifference to our children may also be the consequence of a limited sense of the future that is displayed in our preoccupation with personal pleasure or career advancement. Our society as a whole does not make it easy for parents to be crazy about kids.

Sometimes the difficulties with parenting in the early months have been the result of sex role distinctions in the family. We have for a long time assumed that the mother would be the primary parent. Because of the bonding that naturally occurs between the mother and the child she carries and nurses, fathers often became outsiders. That distance was intensified with industrialization, when a father's work took him out of the home. Moreover it was generally assumed that men, because they were awkward and clumsy, could not be trusted to wash valuable dishes or hold babies. The increased role of fathers in the preparation for birth and the birth itself will diminish some of that distance. Mothers need no longer struggle alone with the heavy burdens of parenting. Fathers can nurture. The emotional interplay in the family context as a whole will be enriched as fathers are able to discover their nurturing capabilities. For this reason when the Church prays for pregnant mothers, it is equally important that it pray for prospective fathers.

We have already noted that the family needs to provide a welcoming environment for the newly born to enter, with time and space for nurturing and the determination to encourage appropriate bonding between parents and children. The family that is able to receive and honor the distinctive gift of the newly born needs to be a hospitable community of ongoing emotional bonds. The shaping of human particularity depends on communities being together in ways that celebrate personal distinctiveness and selfhood. Commitment to being together and commitment to individuation are of equal importance for the family of the newly born.

Baptism, Community, and Autonomy

Baptism is a significant symbol for both aspects of the process by which an individual self is formed. It is a sign of welcoming that transforms a particular family's acceptance into a global belonging. It is a celebration of reception that reinforces and expands a family's welcome. The child who is marked for discipleship with the sign of the Cross is bound to the wider community of Jesus Christ. For the baptized there is never any doubt that they are at home in the world because they belong to God.

The second part of that process focuses on individual autonomy. However, the development of autonomy does not occur in a vacuum nor for its own sake. It requires a hospitable environment in which the unique gifts of each new life are fostered and celebrated. The purpose of the family is to create an environment in which such individuation might occur. Becoming a separate and distinct self is most likely to happen in the context of communities that can love and let go. It is our pastoral task to encourage families to create the kind of hospitable space for the newly born that fosters individual autonomy. Psychological hatching for the baptized is never an end in itself, however. It is always for the sake of discipleship.

Although baptism is primarily a ritual of initiation into the Christian community, it also contributes to the development of human autonomy. To be baptized means to be chosen and named by God as a distinct individual and at the same time to be incorporated into a community that transcends all human particularity. The baptism of infants enhances the development of human autonomy because it is a reminder to parents that the child in their home is theirs and yet not theirs. We let our children go because ultimately they belong to God. And because our children belong to God, it is our responsibility as parents to help them become separate and distinct beings so that they are able to use their gifts for service in the world for Christ's sake. Hence the Rite of Enrollment for Baptism in the next chapter is also a rite celebrating God's election (vocation) of the child to life and service in Christ.

What is ritualized in the ritual of baptism is a truth that transcends the Christian tradition. In *The Prophet* Kahlil Gibran describes this sense that our children do not belong to us:

> And a woman who held a babe against her bosom said, Speak to us of children.
> And he said:
> Your children are not your children.
> They are the sons and daughters of Life's longing for itself.
> They come through you but not from you.
> And though they are with you yet they belong not to you.[3]

From the beginning of each new life, we need to be aware that our children are not our own. Even though they are helpless and dependent and needing food and a supply of raw materials free, they are nonetheless distinct and autonomous creatures of God. We are to nurture our children but not possess them. They do not belong to us because they belong to God.

The establishment of autonomy does not preclude dependence as the norm for human life. This paradoxical connection between autonomy and dependence is intended in the meaning of baptism. The infant is symbolically separated from its maternal world by means of rebirth and initiation into the family of God and at the same time established in a holding environment of the Church in which God's Spirit is present. To be baptized is to be initiated into a covenant with God in which each individual is encouraged to risk standing alone in the presence of God. Parents whose nurturing is informed by this understanding of baptism are likely to foster in their children a lively sense of autonomy in the midst of community.

The development of autonomy is never for its own sake, however. Baptism is initiation into a community that is shaped by the event of Christ, a community that draws its members into ever larger human communities. Baptism is the beginning of a discipleship that demands our ultimate loyalty. The family and the Church are contexts that nurture each individual's gifts in such a way that they can be used for service in the world for Christ's sake. Baptism is a reminder to parents to encourage their children to become autonomous disciples of the Gospel.

Naming and Baptism

The paradox of individuation and participation that governs our understanding of the significance of baptism in the course of human development is equally applicable to the process of naming. We are particularized by our name and located within a specific community. Our name is the locus of perceiving, feeling, acting and being acted upon, valuing and being valued. It is also the means by which we identify ourselves in relation to other persons and things. My name is my own, but it is also the symbol of my participation in community.[4]

How we are named is therefore a significant factor in the formation of a self. Even the most casual and random naming of a child is not without influence on that child's life. However, it is less what the child is named than it is the parental expectations that accompany the name that are really important. There is no magic in the name itself, but there is real influence in the expectations of the parents that the child will become what he or she is called.

> Marlys and Donald Hopkins had a splendid courtship. During a particularly happy occasion they decided, quite innocently, to name their first daughter Joy. It was a name that came out of their experience, but it carried with it expectations of the child. Eventually they had a daughter and they named her Joy. When Joy was a teenager, however, she had to struggle against depression, a depression she did not feel she was free to have or about which she was free to talk to her parents. It seemed to her that it would be easier to change her name than to alter the expectation, which she had internalized from her parents, that Joy is always joyful. She did not dislike her name, but she felt confined by the expectations that went with it.

It was not their conscious intention to limit her freedom to be sad or depressed by naming her Joy. Likewise parents who name their children for a deceased relative may not expect that child to turn out as an exact replica. Nor are children named for real or fictional persons of eminence expected to achieve a similar fame. However, it is important that parents be aware that a child's experience of his or her name may exceed the parents' conscious intent. Attention to the possible impact of a given name will certainly enhance the uniqueness of the individual person.

Naming a child after a relative serves to locate the child within the history of the particular family. It is a gesture of solidarity with that relative. It is also a symbolic way of linking the child with an emotionally significant part of his or her past.

Evon Olive is bound to her mother and grandmother in very special ways. Evon is her mother's middle name and Olive is her maternal grandmother's first name. Her name set Evon apart from the other women in her family, all of whom had first and second names beginning with E. Moreover grandmother Olive was a particularly loving person. Everyone felt special, unique, loved, and enjoyed in her presence. Later in life Evon acknowledged the importance of her relationship to her grandmother. "Olive has come to represent all the unconditional love and compassion my grandmother had for me and I for her. I sign my name 'Evon O.' for her remembrance. I have consciously incorporated the attributes that I loved so much in my grandmother into my own being."

Being named for her mother and grandmother was a confirmation of belonging for Evon. It fulfilled the symbolic function of embodying in her the continuity of the generations. She did not need to make a name for herself because she had been given a name that already has a history. To be named for a relative establishes the child in the family from the beginning. Yet there is a danger that in naming a child for a relative, there will be an emphasis on continuity and belonging at the expense of individuation and autonomy. Sarah Beth felt the latter keenly. Both her brother and her sister were named for relatives from both families of origin: Sarah's sister, Carolyn, was named for her mother's sister and her brother, William, was named after his father. Sarah Beth was named for no one. In contrast to her siblings, Sarah had no difficulty leaving home and establishing her independence, but freedom to be autonomous was hers only at the expense of a sense of belonging.

If naming is a means whereby we are located within a specific community, then it is important that the name given in baptism be a Christian name. In some ethnic communities religious tradition requires that the names Mary and Joseph precede any other name given to the child. In the 1576 folio edition of the Geneva Bible there is a list of proper names, chiefly from the Old Testament, accompanied by the following admonition:

We haue nowe set forth this table of the names that be most vsed in the olde Testament with their interpretations, as the Hebrew importeth, partly to call backe the godly from that abuse, when they shall knowe the true names of the Godly Fathers and what they signifie, that their children nowe named after them may haue testimonies by their very name that they are within that faythfull familie, that in all their doing had ever God before their eyes, and that they are bounde by theie names to serve God from their infancie, and haue occasion to praise him for his workes wrought in them and their fathers.

The name given at baptism not only identifies a child within a particular human family, but also locates that child within the family of God. It is like a string tied around the finger to remind us to whom we belong and whom we are bound to serve from infancy. The name given at baptism connotes the incorporation into the family of God and remains forever as a testimony of that identity.

Our response to our children should from the beginning maximize their freedom to develop their own gifts. The expectations of parents, more than the name itself, may limit the development of that uniqueness. Consequently in working with couples before the rite of enrollment, it is appropriate and necessary to explore with them the significance of the child's name. The point of raising the subject of the child's name is to help parents become aware of the ways in which expectations carried by the name might restrict the development of the child's own unique way of being in the world. Our pastoral conversations with parents prior to baptism should examine how the names they have chosen for their child will both symbolize the fact that the child belongs to significant communities, such as Church and family, *and* enhance the process of individuation.

Birth in a Believing Environment

There is a reciprocity between the rituals which initiate a child into a family and infant baptism, which is the ritual of initiation into the family of God. Both processes mediate between the needs of the individual and the needs of the community. Both processes of initiation maintain a delicate balance between continuity and change. They form a bridge between the past and the future. Rituals of initiation like baptism provide a framework and a symbolic presentation for the processes of transformation that confirm our uniqueness *and* transpose us into a context in which our vision of humanity is always expanding. We have sought to illuminate this relationship between ritual and life, between event and process, so that the process of initiation lived out in specific families informs the ritual of baptism and so that families are aware from a sacramental perspective what is at stake in the ordinary events by which a family welcomes a child.

The child that is welcomed into a family is enabled to feel at home in the world. Without that welcome, as we saw, there is always the sense that love is conditional and belonging is tentative.

The child's first experience of the world's hospitality is in the family. Therefore it is critical for human development and for faith that the infant is welcomed into a hospitable environment in which love abounds. The family as a community of persons "finds in love the source and the constant impetus for welcoming, respecting and promoting each one of its members in his or her lofty dignity as a person, that is, as a living image of God."[5] The child who is baptized is doubly welcomed.

The communities into which our children are initiated are holding environments that are to protect and nourish for the sake of growth in autonomy. A holding environment is crazy about kids. "In the family, which is a community of persons, special attention must be devoted to the children by developing a profound esteem for their personal dignity and a great respect and generous concern for their right."[6] Acceptance, love, esteem, freedom, safety, affection, respect, and many-sided material, emotional, educational, and spiritual concern for each child should always characterize a holding environment that is faithful to Christ's command to "let the children come to me." Baptism is a symbolic reminder to parents that they are to hold their children in order to let them go. Our children are not our children even when we love and protect and honor them as our own because by baptism they have been initiated into a community of love and obligation that transcends the human family. The family and the Church are both "cradles" of protection and nurture that hold us for service in the world.

HAVING A CHILD AS AN ACT OF FAITH

The family and the Church are welcoming and holding environments that make hospitable space for human growth in life and faith. They are also believing environments whose actions are signs of faithfulness. Each family is a witness to the love of God in Christ Jesus. By the ways they respond to a child and by virtue of their ministry of educating, parents are the first heralds of the Gospel for their children. The family is a believing environment by virtue of its decision to have or adopt a child; it is a believing environment by the ways in which it engenders trust and hope in its children; and it is a believing environment because its life always points beyond itself to Christ and the world for which Christ died.

The decision to have a child is itself an act of Christian faithfulness. It is an expression of trust that God will keep the promise that we will not be abandoned in the future that is being made. It is a demonstration of willingness to cooperate with God in the creation of a future for humanity. The decision to have a child is the beginning of a shift away from the primacy of the marital bond toward a larger vision of generations past and future. Couples who are unable to have children need to realign their relationship to include a wider community, not only to serve the world but to protect the marriage from stagnation. Even though it can be said that the addition of children brings vitality to a family's life, that alone cannot be the reason for having children.

Some people who marry today are reluctant to have children because the future seems so bleak to them. It seems futile and unnecessarily painful to bring children into a world that seems bent on its own destruction. Given the vulnerability of the human community in a nuclear age, it is no longer simply a question of whether our children will have faith when they grow up, but whether they will have a future at all. In that context it is appropriate for us to ask if our *faith* will have children. Having children is rooted in the conviction that God may give us a future for which we do not plan or contrive. Because the future is filled with uncertainty, it is only by faith that we will have children. And because our children are born into a world whose future is clouded by the possibility of annihilation, it is a matter of survival that they be formed by communities of hope.

The birth of a child is a precious gift in the midst of the discontinuities of the world. Our faith will have children in spite of those discontinuities. Such birth is a mighty and painful labor. The child given us by faith is never an easy birth, but it is a birth for which we wait in eager longing because it is a sign that God continues to make all things new.

Having or adopting a child is an act of faith because the gift of a child is always filled with surprise. No matter how much the newly born may resemble his or her parents, no matter how we might even be able to determine certain characteristics through genetic manipulation, the birth of a child is still a gift from God that is always a surprise. It is an act of unfaith to reject a child who does not match our expectations or to circumscribe a child's development in such a way that the child's unique gifts are kept hidden. With each child God is "making a new thing" for eyes of faith to see.

By welcoming a child into its midst, the family is embarking on a faith journey because it cannot ever anticipate how it will be affected by the addition of a child. The family is always changed in surprising ways when children are added. The family's capacity to adapt to that new life and the changes it always brings is a sign of its vitality and an act of faithfulness. It is, however, never easy. The changes that families need to make to adapt to the "new thing that God is doing" are usually more difficult *and* more rewarding than we expect. Families sin when they rigidly hold to fixed patterns of interacting that force the child to conform to the system that is already in place. The result is that the child's freedom to discover his or her gifts for the world is restricted by the family's need for familiarity and safety. Having a child is a journey in faith filled with surprises.

The Birth of Faith, Hope, and Love

The birth of a child and the baptism of a child are occasions for parents and local assemblies of Christians to renew their faith. As part of their preparation for the baptism of a child, parents reaffirm their life in the Church and affirm their commitment to nurture the baptized child in the Christian faith. The child is initiated into a particular assembly of people, who remember the mighty acts of God and continue to live out a promise that God still acts for people today. The faith of the Christian community becomes the wider context for baptism. One might say that the infant has faith because the community means his or her baptism. Within the assembly the baptism of infants is a reminder that everyone is eligible for the gift that is given and received by grace in baptism.

Although there is no way to guarantee that the child will claim the particular faith into which he or she has been baptized, the community's faith is transmitted to infants in the form of basic trust. Erik Erikson has made a creative link between faith and the basic trust of infancy. "Religion, it seems, is the oldest and has been the most lasting institution to serve the ritual restoration of a sense of trust in the form of faith while offering a tangible formula for a sense of evil against which it promises to arm and defend humankind."[7] The basic trust that is transmitted by hospitable, nurturing communities represents a common grace to which is added the special grace of baptism.

The presence of the Holy Spirit in and from baptism not only prevents the baptismal life from becoming a meaningless routine, but it also guarantees to the baptized the presence of a Power that activates and reinforces the child's basic trust in the world's trustworthiness. It is impossible to separate the emergence of faith from the infant's experience of the trustworthiness of the nurturers. However, parents are not trustworthy all the time, and some parents are hardly ever worthy of trust. The community's faith into which a child is baptized is a gift from God that transforms and transcends each infant's experience of the world. In that sense the genesis of both faith and trust belong to the mystery of God.

Of all the virtues and values that develop in humankind, hope is the first, the most basic, and the most lasting. It is, as Erik Erikson has suggested, the indispensable virtue of life. The psychological source of hope depends on the infant's first encounter with "trustworthy maternal persons." If this encounter satisfies the infant's need for intake and contact, if the ratio between trust and mistrust is favorable, and if there is a mutuality of response between the infant and the mothering one, then the fundamental human strength of hope is established. In order for this hope to emerge, basic trust must outweigh basic mistrust in the psychosocial crisis of infancy.

Because of this intimate connection between faith and basic trust in infancy, it is important that preparation for the baptism of a child attend both to the parents' affirmation of the Christian faith *and* their attitude of trust in the world. It is difficult for children to discover the gift of faith from parents whose stance toward the world is filled with doubt and suspicion and fear. Whether our children will have faith and be faithful persons in the world depends on their experience of trustworthiness and faithfulness in the earliest nurturing communities of family and Church.

In the same way that trust in the parent is necessary for infant hope, so also hope is inseparable from trust in God whose love is constant. In both instances the origin of hope is *extra nos.* The hope that is engendered in infancy by an experience of trustworthy nurturance is for the Christian undergirded by the covenant character of God. It is rooted in the dependable nature of God, who keeps faith with people of any time and place. The Christian is initiated into this covenant of living hope through baptism. "By his great mercy, we have been born anew to a living hope through the resurrection of Jesus Christ from the dead" (1 Pet 1:3). Hope is the consequence of rebirth. This new birth through baptism is initiation into a community that is ultimately rooted in the dependability of God. However, unless that hope is at least partially verified by the ordinary love and trustworthiness of nurturing parents, it will not mature. Unless the hope born in the infant through the trustworthiness of parents is further grounded in the One who orders and sustains all of life, it will not endure.

The family is the first and most fundamental school for social living. It is a community in which we learn the art of self-giving love from the sacrificial love of parents.

> In a society shaken and split by tensions and conflicts caused by the violent clash of various kinds of individualism and selfishness, children must be enriched not only with a sense of true justice, which alone leads to respect for the personal dignity of each individual, but also and more powerfully by a sense of true love, understood as sincere solicitude and disinterested service with regard to others, especially the poorest and those in most need.[8]

The baptism of infants is a sign that no one, not even the children, are excluded from God's love. It obligates parents to regard their children from the beginning of life as fully human, unique, and surprising creations of God, who are subjects as well as objects of love. The natural bonds of flesh and blood should engender the interior strength of love that eventually enables us to care for larger and larger human communities.

BAPTIZED TO SERVE

It should be clear by now that the Church's preparation of parents for the baptism of their children needs to be concerned with their faithfulness in responding to the needs of the newly born as well as with the faith of the believing community into which the child is baptized. Preparation for parenthood and preparation for infant baptism are interdependent. Both require a reorientation of focus. Parenthood is first of all an act of altruism. Although there are parenting skills to be learned, the task of the Church is to help people recover the *vocation* of parenthood. Fathers and mothers parent best when they are able to be attentive primarily to the needs of the infant. The baptism of infants is a paradigm of parental care because it welcomes a child into a hospitable environment but always insists on letting the child go for the sake of service in the world.

The baptism of infants contributes to the development of human autonomy because it reminds parents that they are caretakers and not possessors of their children. We are to love, honor, protect, and respect our children from the beginning of life so that they might become autonomous enough to serve the world for the sake of Christ. Although the Church's ministry with those preparing for the birth and baptism of a child will take a variety of expressions, the purpose is the same: to help the family create the kind of welcoming environment for the newly born that will foster individual growth in autonomy in the midst of community. The ritual of baptism is shaped by the same paradox of individual autonomy and community participation that determines the formation of the self. Baptism, as a second birth into a second holding environment, initiates a child into a process in which both family and Church are determined to mediate the life of faith and life of grace for the child. In introducing the newly arrived child into these believing environments, the parents and others undertake a profoundly religious reponsibility, a responsibility which will draw upon and test their own effective participation in the life of the one Body and their sharing in the prophetic, priestly, and royal ministries that Christ continues to exercise through those who believe in his name.

Implications for Ministry

The following ministry suggestions, it will be noted, begin before the events of birth and baptism and point beyond those events to the processes of human renewal which unfold the meaning of baptism throughout the human life cycle:

• In a broad sense the preparation for the addition of a child begins with the processes by which a man and woman leave father and mother in order to form a new family. If there is space in the togetherness of the marital pair, it is likely that there will be room for the child. How we help people get married, therefore, is a crucial beginning for the tasks of parenting.

• Having children has always been an intentional act, even though precise knowledge of the procreative process is relatively recent. Couples who marry today face choices not available or necessary a century ago. Since biological accident can no longer be equated automatically with God's will, questions about having children and commitments to nurture children need to be part of premarital work. Because it can no longer be assumed that mothers will necessarily be the primary nurturer of the child, so deciding who will have the main responsibility for raising the children must be part of the decision to have children at all. The diversity of childrearing options today has made it increasingly important for the marital couple to consider explicitly what their respective expectations are concerning parenting roles.

• Couples wishing to have children but physically impeded from doing so need the support and prayers of the Christian community in overcoming those impediments. Childless couples who wish to have children by artificial means face a labyrinth of complicated ethical questions created by the new reproductive technologies. It is the Church's task to continue to reexamine its own moral and theological principles as medical technology continues to develop. Nevertheless, it must also be said that having children is a gift, not a right. Because couples are often eager to use any means to overcome impediments to childbearing, the Church's task is to mediate between ethical understandings and psychological consequences for each individual, for families, and for the larger human community.

• The mother has a particular responsibility to provide as hospitable a womb as possible, and pregnant women exercise this responsibility chiefly by being careful about their bodies. At a minimum this means the avoidance of smoking, the moderate consumption of alcoholic beverages, and extreme care in the use of drugs of any kind. Some have extended their concern for the mother's body as a hospitable space to include psychological and intellectual well-being. One woman, for example, read Dr. Seuss books to her yet unborn child as part of a prenatal stimulation program. A Dr. Seuss story was read at birth, so it is said, and the child did not cry. The mother concluded that "it made her [the baby girl] feel like she was at home." Although this sort of activity may seem rather farfetched, we really do not know the impact of environmental factors on the unborn child, though we are by now very well aware that a proper environment is crucial to the child *after* birth. Including pregnant mothers and expectant fathers in the weekly prayers of the faithful is one way in which the Church can help prospective parents become aware of how important it is during pregnancy to make room, in all sorts of ways, for the coming child. Forming journal groups or support groups of expectant parents for prayer, reflection and mutual encouragement is another way to foster a holding environment (see Gail Ramshaw-Schmidt, "Ritual Before Birth," below, pp. 140–143).

• Pastoral conversation with families where there are already children needs to provide the children, too, with the opportunity not only to express reservations about the new addition, but to think about what they would like to contribute to the yet-to-be-born child. Each family member might be asked to identify a personal characteristic he or she would like to be able to pass on to the new baby. This is a simple way of engaging all the members of a family in the process of making room for the child and offering hospitality to that child. It is also a way of making explicit influences that might otherwise remain implicit.

• Visitation at the hospital or home at the time of the birth is usually an occasion for celebration. It is an occasion to celebrate the absolute and wonderful uniqueness of each and every human life. It is an occasion to celebrate and affirm the "craziness" about children which makes it possible for parents to endure messy diapers and mashed squash on the TV screen and the smell of baby powder throughout the house. The pastor, joining in the general praise of the wonderfulness of the child, thereby participates in a process that begins to meet the child's need for affirmation and love. Sometimes, however, such postpartum visitation is a time of sadness rather than celebration. The death of an infant or the birth of a child with serious deformities or disabilities is very difficult to accept. But there are situations of grief or nonacceptance surrounding the birth of a child where the reactions seem, on the surface at least, quite inappropriate. Effective pastoral care will always be alert to the presence of such situations.

• An increasing number of mothers and fathers are choosing something other than standard hospital childbirth, such as opting to give birth at home or in a birthing center. Such options have the particular advantage of making the whole family much more aware of the importance of its role in welcoming the newborn. For its part the Church, insofar as it has the ability to influence health care systems, should be working to promote everything that would contribute to humanizing the birth process without endangering the well-being of mother and child. This could mean working with hospitals to make them a more humane environment in which to welcome the newborn into the world. It may mean encouraging parents to have children at home. But it could also mean working in the larger society towards those changes in work patterns which would make it possible for those who work outside the home to spend more time with their children.

• The Rite of Enrollment for Baptism (below, pp. 146–148) offers an opportunity to make explicit the significance of the names chosen for a child. It is also the occasion to rehearse, at least in the family circle, the account of the child's birth. Such stories are a significant part of a family's mythology. These stories also embody impressions and expectations that influence our response to a child.

In some cultures a name given to the child reflects the circumstances or nature of that child's birth. Telling the birth story in conjunction with the rite of naming is one way to enhance the uniqueness of the child from the beginning.

• The preparation of parents for the baptism of a child provides an opportunity to emphasize the importance of the vocation of parenthood. It is an occasion in which to explore with fathers and mothers the necessity of altruism for successful parenting. It is a time to alert prospective parents to the importance of empathy in nurturing children. There is no higher calling for Christians than to nurture our young to become responsible and faithful members of the people of God. As Andrew Thompson has indicated, the attitude of the family towards the world and the way they embody their Christian faith in a faithful life-style serve to create a hospitable environment within which a child will be encouraged to develop his or her own faith life.

• Baptism is more than a family affair. It is initiation into a community that calls every individual to a widening arena of concern. Baptism is a sign to parents that their children are not their children, for they belong to God who has called them into existence and calls them into service of the world. Helping parents understand from the beginning that their children belong to God for the sake of the world will help ensure that the children have a chance to develop as autonomous human beings. Sponsorship serves the same end. Whether the congregation as a whole or specific individuals are the sponsors or godparents is less important than the symbolic function of sponsorship: in baptism the child is incorporated into a larger family which both promises and demands loyalty. Baptism is the beginning of a life of discipleship, which demands to be given priority over any and all other loyalties. The promise given in baptism is that God will not abandon us on the way. The family and the Church in turn are two contexts in which we may discover the faithfulness of God and so nurture our gifts for the world that we can also give them away.

• From a Christian perspective parenting is more than a duty. It is a privilege and a responsibility. The mother's womb provides a safe, hospitable environment in which the child may prepare for birth. During the same time the family is making its own preparations. For several years following birth the family has to serve as a hospitable space in which the child may prepare for autonomous life and for service to the world. Throughout this time the Church has the responsibility for supporting and enhancing these ordinary life systems for the sake of future generations.

• Like the family the Church is a holding environment for the process of human growth and development. Children and parents hold on to each other until it is time to let go; so it is with the Church. The Church has to embrace the young until they are old enough to assume their Christian responsibilities in the world. One way of holding the young, common in some traditions, is the "cradle roll," a public listing of the baptized children whom the parish holds and nurtures and prays for. Such a practice keeps the parish aware of its responsibilities for those whom it baptizes. Another such "holding environment," of course, is the parochial school.

Baptism is a process as well as an event. The meaning of baptism extends through the whole human life cycle. The rite of baptism, although momentary, is complete in itself; the baptized child is incorporated into the life of the Church and thus into the life of Christ. Yet the entire Christian life is nothing less than the living out of what transpires in baptism. What is appropriated at various crisis points in the cycle of life is already given in baptism. Thus it can be said that the Christian life is a daily baptism which once begun continues to unfold through life and death.

Footnotes

1. Robert L. Browning and Roy A. Reed, *The Sacraments in Religious Education and Liturgy* (Birmingham: Religious Education Press, 1985) 92.

2. W. H. Auden, "Mundus et Infans," *Selected Poetry of W. H. Auden*, 2nd ed. (New York: Vintage Books, 1971) 76.

3. Kahlil Gibran *The Prophet* (New York: Knopf, 1966) 17.

4. Recognition of the symbolic importance of naming prompted the Roman Catholic Church to make specific provision for a first public naming of the child at the moment of its being welcomed to the Church. See *Rite of Baptism for Children* (1969) n. 37.

5. John Paul II, *On the Family* (Washington: U. S. Catholic Conference, 1982) 20.

6. *Ibid.* 26.

7. Erik H. Erikson, *Identity: Youth and Crisis* (New York: Norton, 1968) 106.

8. John Paul II, *On the Family*, 37.

4. CELEBRATING BAPTISM IN STAGES: A PROPOSAL

Gail Ramshaw-Schmidt

Introduction

Since its issue the Rite of Christian Initiation for Adults has been a significant source of renewal in the Church. Yet for much of the Christianized world, infant baptism remains the expected procedure, and there has not been sufficient thought given recently to the rituals surrounding the baptism of infants. Infants are now given an abbreviated rite which uses elements logically appropriate only for adults. This proposal affirms that the grace of God saves human children even before they as conscious adults reject sin and accept God. This proposal uses biblical images, besides the death and resurrection of Christ, which are particularly amenable to the baptism of infants, as well as offering home and church rituals before and after baptism which attend to the family context of infant baptism.

The Scriptures are full of stories of the very young being saved by God: Noah's children and the dumb animals saved from the flood; Isaac snatched away from sacrifice; Ishmael rescued from death; Joseph retrieved from the pit; Moses guarded by Miriam; Samuel offered as a toddler; David anointed as a boy; the widow's son revived by Elijah; the eschatological call to even nursing infants; the children blessed by Jesus; Jarius' daughter raised; the Syrophoenician woman's daughter healed; Timothy reared in the faith. Many of these stories narrate a child's passage from death to life. Thus the Paschal theme, more than some might assume, is explicitly appropriate to children. But there is more than narrative. For while Christian theology has followed Paul in explicating baptism primarily as a paschal incorporation into the death and resurrection of Christ, the Scriptures offer other images for baptism which are more amenable to infants.

There is the Johannine passage of the second birth (John 4), which suggests a picture of the baptismal water as the nurturing waters of the womb of God. There is the Pauline analogy of baptism to adoption as children of God (Rom 8) as well as Paul's explication of baptism as incorporation into the body of Christ, which is the community of believers (1 Cor 12). In baptism we drink God's milk (Isa 49); we are washed from stain (Acts 2); we receive the name of Christ indelibly on our forehead (Rev 14); we are anointed to be heirs in the royal family (1 Peter 2); we are clothed with the garments of God (Eph 6); and, reusing one of the most common images for baptism in the ancient Church, we are illuminated by the light of God (John 9). The monster churning up the waters is the monster also inside the human soul, and our faith that in this infant we will see the mysterious salvation of God is appropriately ritualized in infant baptism. Infant baptism is not so much Pasch as Pentecost, the infusion of God's Holy Spirit into this infant human being.

If we think of the Christian life as concluding at death, then the idea of the adult catechumenate, the adult Christian consciously choosing Christ in maturity, is attractive. When, however, we think eschatologically of God's reign coming to fruition only in the end time and yet also being mystically present in all the baptized, infant baptism becomes much more intriguing. For the reign of God is hardly to be equated with even the mature Christian commitment. Indeed, the infant and the saintly old woman are closer to one another than either is to God. It is clear that, despite this, adult images for the Christian life are at present dominant. We speak of regeneration, deliverance from an old life, the brothers and sisters of the *koinonia*, conversion, and redemption—all terms which flatter us with our maturity. Yet there are the alternative images: formation, delivery from a womb, the sons and daughters of Mother Church, nurture, and divinization—images which construe us all with our infants as helpless before the mystery of God.

Yet when we have granted that infant baptism is a legitimate alternative mode of the reception of grace, and as we sit down to shape such a ritual to be in fact more amenable to infants, we acknowledge that the infant is to a terrifying degree the product of a family environment. Of course adults as well reflect their household and its values in their commitments and causes. But we see the dependence on household more clearly for the infant. If children are to come to public worship, their guardians must bring them. If they are to learn the stories of the faith and are to incorporate the Church's symbols into their days, the family must provide at least the raw materials. One hears that in Sweden children are baptized in the maternity wards and that Church membership has no relation to baptism. To avoid such crises, indiscriminate baptism and lack of nurture must be addressed. There is great pastoral responsibility to see that the households of baptized children have some understanding of what baptism is and that they commit themselves to raising the child in the faith. The Church will have a difficult job preaching the centrality of baptism if in practice baptism is automatically available on a moment's notice to anyone remotely connected with the Church.

Thus it is expedient to entertain a rite of Christian initiation for infants. Such a rite will value infant baptism as a sign of God's grace and will probe for scriptural imagery of Pentecostal rebirth, at the same time taking seriously the catechesis of the infant's family as the matrix for the child's mystagogy. The RCIA proposes a "journey of faith" for adults which progresses in four stages: Precatechumenate, Catechumenate, the Lenten period of Enlightenment and Purification, and the period of Mystagogy. The rituals of the RCIA are of two kinds: those which mark the transitions between the stages (the Rite of Becoming a Catechumen, the Rite of Enrollment or Election, the Easter Sacraments); and those which accompany the candidates during each stage (exorcisms, blessings, scrutinies, presentations). These stages have their equivalents in the proposed Rite of Infant Baptism in Stages, beginning before the child's birth and moving on through birth and baptism into the lifelong process of mystagogy. For each stage and for the transitions between stages, rites are suggested which are appropriate to the faith journey of the family and of the wider Christian community as they receive the child from God and assume the responsibility under God for that child's life in the Spirit.

In outline the journey is as follows:

Stage One: Precatechumenate
  A. Ritual Before Birth
  B. Rite of Baptismal Intent

Stage Two: Catechumenate
    C. Ritual After Birth
    D. Ritual After Death
    E. Rite of Enrollment

Stage Three: Purification and Illumination
    F. Prayer Before Baptism
    G. Rite of Christian Baptism for Children

Stage Four: Mystagogy
    H. Baptismal Remembrance at Church
    I. Baptismal Remembrance at Home

STAGE ONE: PRECATECHUMENATE

Ritual Before Birth

The purpose of a ritual before birth is to attend to the complex feelings of expectant parents. The context could be a home visitation or a group meeting of expectant parents. The rite could also be used as part of family prayer in the weeks before the child is due. Whether conducted by the clergy, by lay leaders, by a journey group of parents, or by family members themselves, this conversation focuses on the spiritual needs of the adults in this life-changing event and on the anticipated faith of the coming child. Such counseling and catechesis centered in prayer implies a parish organization which identifies expectant parents, a pastoral situation which involves the whole community in the joys and sorrows of its members, and a willingness to face the ambivalent feelings of expectant parents. Some pregnancies are wanted, others are not; some parents and families see new life as a gift, others see it as a threat; some have a clear sense of their identity as a Christian home, others do not. The parents should be helped to anticipate the coming child, to think about their role as Christian parents, and to review the meaning of Christian baptism. That such a visit or meeting culminate in prayer, the following "Ritual Before Birth" is suggested as a culminating prayer.

Leader: Our help is in the name of the Lord.

All: The maker of heaven and earth.

> Glory be to the Father and to the Son and to the Holy Spirit as it was in the beginning, is now, and ever shall be, world without end. Amen.

A psalm is recited together, antiphonally or responsorially:

Ps 103   We praise God for blessing us throughout life.
Ps 86   We beg God to preserve our life from danger.
Ps 113   We praise God who gives life to the human race.

A lesson is read:

Judg 13:2-8   Samson's parents are told of the coming birth.
Luke 1:5-17   John is promised as an ambassador of God's love.
Luke 2:39-56 Elizabeth and Mary rejoice in their pregnancies as gifts from God.

A brief period of reflection and prayer may follow.

Leader: Let us offer our prayers to God.

For . . . , let us pray to the Lord.

All: Lord, have mercy.

All are invited to offer petitions. The following may be useful in certain circumstances:

> That the coming child may be healthy and whole, let us pray . . . .
>
> That the child may prove a blessing to the world . . . .
>
> That the child's father, mother, brothers and sisters may be blessed with peace . . . .
>
> That with courage, faith and gratefulness we may renew our commitment as a Christian family . . . .
>
> That N., the mother of the child, may be granted safe pregnancy and a normal labor . . . .

Leader: Our Father . . . .

The leader signs the cross on the mother's forehead, saying:

> May the Lord bless you and keep you,
> bringing you safely
> to your child's birth and baptism.

All: Amen.

Leader: Let us bless the Lord.

All: Thanks be to God.

Rite of Baptismal Intent

The purpose of the Rite of Baptismal Intent, which corresponds to the Rite for the Making of a Catechumen in the RCIA, is to make public before the Christian community the parents' commitment to raise their children as Christians. This rite is the liturgical event which culminates a process of instruction, reflection, and prayer expected of Christian parents. Such a process includes both pastoral attention to the spiritual needs of the adults as they enter parenthood and also catechetical instruction for their own faith and for the sake of the anticipated faith of the child. That the ecclesial dimensions of this process might be manifested and that the parents' faith commitment be ritualized within the Sunday assembly, the family several weeks before the expected arrival (by birth or adoption) are presented before the final blessing by a sponsor or parish representative, who personifies the link between the family and the wider Church.

Before the final blessing, the sponsor presents the family to the congregation, saying:

I present the *N.* family.
Anticipating the arrival of a new child,
they are here to declare their intention
to have their child baptized.

Presider (to family):

What do you ask of God's Church?

Family: Faith.

Presider: What does faith offer you?

Family: Eternal life.

Presider: For whom do you ask such faith?

Leader: For the child to come.

Presider: God gives grace to all who seek it.
We await with joy the baptism of your child.

If the rite takes place in a context other than that of a Sunday assembly with its own liturgy of the Word, a lesson is read:

Deut 30:15-20   Moses urges the people to choose life for their children.

2 Tim 1:3-14   Paul praises God for Timothy's rearing by his Christian mother and grandmother.

The presider may speak briefly to the specific situation. Then, with hand outstretched over the family, he prays:

> Again and again in ages past, O God,
> you have saved the children whom you love.
>
> The infant Moses you snatched from death
> with the help of his mother and his sister.
>
> You accepted Samuel while yet a toddler,
> Hannah his mother singing for joy.
>
> As you blessed Mary with your Spirit,
> bless also this family,
> that, renewed in their own baptismal life,
> they may welcome as a sign of your love
> the child you send.
>
> May the child live to receive baptism
> and mature in this household,
> enlivened by the Spirit of your Son,
> Jesus Christ our Lord.

All: Amen.

The presider blesses the mother with the Sign of the Cross, saying:

> The Lord bless you and keep you,
> bringing you safely
> to your child's birth and baptism.

All: Amen.

The final blessing and dismissal of the people follow.

STAGE TWO: CATECHUMENATE

Ritual After Birth

The purpose of a visit after birth, either at the hospital or at the home, is to deal pastorally with the birth, to plan for the Rite of Enrollment, and to discuss baptism further. The birth may have been happy and healthy, in which case the object of the visit is to thank God and to anticipate baptism. This would be the logical time to discuss with parents the child's name, if this has not been done earlier, and to explore the expectations implied by that choice. The parents are to be encouraged in their role as the first catechists of the child and to see the Christian home as a microchurch and a nursery of the faith.

The birth may have been unhappy or tragic. The child may be unwanted or impaired. In this case the object of the visit would be to pray for God's blessing in a difficult situation and for the parish to offer itself as a support community for the distressed or bewildered parents. Preparing to enroll the child for baptism will be a pledge of such support and a sign of the free grace of God.

To culminate the visit in prayer, the Ritual After Birth is suggested. Care must be taken to choose the psalm, lessons, and petitions to fit the specific situation.

Leader: Our help is in the name of the Lord.

All: The maker of heaven and earth.

Glory be to the Father . . . .

A psalm is read, antiphonally or responsorially:

Ps 113 God is praised for the gift of the child.
Ps 145 The generations praise God, helper of those in need.

A lesson is read:

1 Sam 1:2–2:10 Hannah praises God for the birth of Samuel.
Luke 2:46-55 Mary sings praises to God for her child.

A brief period of reflection and prayer may follow.

Leader: Let us offer our prayers to God.
For . . . , let us pray to the Lord.

All: Lord, have mercy.

All are invited to offer petitions. The following may be useful in certain circumstances:

In joy and delight at the birth of this child,
let us pray . . . .

That the child may be kept safe until the day of his/her baptism . . . .

That we may be strengthened to live as a Christian family . . . .

That we may embrace this child with the loving arms of God's people . . . .

That, like flowing milk, God's mercy will fill us all with life . . . .

That, in spite of her/his weakness, *N.* may live to
    praise God and to be a blessing to others . . . .

That we may be given the grace to open our hearts
    to this child . . . .

All: Our Father, who art in heaven . . . .

The leader lays hands on the child's head, saying

The Lord bless you and keep you
until the day of your baptism.

Leader: Let us bless the Lord.

All: Thanks be to God.

Ritual After Death

The mother may have had a miscarriage or a still birth. The baby may have died unbaptized shortly after birth. The family may be appealing for pastoral care after an abortion. In such situations, the visitors must be pastorally sensitive to the family's complex feelings and offer them compassion from the Lord. The family must be lifted out of sorrow and guilt and into the peace of the children of God. That such a visit culminate in prayer, Ritual After Death is suggested.

Leader: Our help is in the name of the Lord.

All: The maker of heaven and earth.

Glory be to the Father . . . .

A psalm is read together, antiphonally or responsorially:

Ps 42 We hope for God's help in time of trouble.
Ps 90 We bless the Lord, the God of life and death.

A lesson is read:

Luke 8:40-42, 49-56 Jesus calls the death of Jairus' daughter a sleep.
Luke 7:11-16   Jesus raises from death the son of the widow
                    of Naim.

A brief period of reflection or word of consolation and hope may follow.

Leader: Let us offer our prayers to God.

For . . . . , let us pray to the Lord.

All: Lord, have mercy.

All are invited to offer petitions. The following may be useful in certain circumstances.

> That God will finish the work of creation begun in this child and bring him/her to the fullness of life, let us pray . . . .
>
> That our child who lived among us so short a time may live forever in the joy of the Lord, let us pray . . . .
>
> That the family may be comforted by the hope of the resurrection, let us pray . . . .
>
> That we may be forgiven our sin and released from remorse, let us pray . . . .
>
> That we may sit together with N. and our whole family at the heavenly banquet, feasting forever on the life of God, let us pray . . . .

All: Our Father, who art in heaven . . . .

Leader: The Lord gives, the Lord takes away.

All: Blessed be the name of the Lord.

Rite of Enrollment or Election

The purpose of the Rite of Enrollment is publicly to enroll the child for baptism and to celebrate its vocation or election to the Christian life. The rite is the liturgical event which recognizes the joy of new children, names the child, praises God for the child, enrolls the child by its given Christian name as one who is to receive baptism, and allows the parents and family to commit themselves to be the child's first community of faith. Because these are ecclesial matters, events of importance to the community and involving the family precisely as members of the Church, they should be ritualized within the Sunday assembly, as soon after the baby's birth as possible. Before the final blessing the family comes forward, accompanied if possible by the prospective godparents.

Before the final blessing, the family presents itself to the assembly:

Parent(s): We offer praise to God at the birth of our child and enroll his/her name as one awaiting baptism.

Presider: What do you ask of God's Church?

Family:	Faith.
Presider:	What does faith offer you?
Family:	Eternal life.
Presider:	For whom do you ask such faith?
Parent(s):	Our child, *N.*
Presider:	Do you offer yourselves as the first community of faith for this child, promising to bring him/her to the services of God's house, to instruct him/her in the life of faith, and to pray for his/her growth in grace?
Family:	We do.

If the rite takes place in a context other than that of a Sunday assembly with its own liturgy of the Word, a lesson is read:

Jer 1:4-10   Jeremiah has been called while yet unborn to be dedicated to God.

Luke 2:22-38 Jesus is presented to God on the eighth day and the onlookers give praise to God.

The presider may speak to the specific situation. Then, with hand outstretched over the child, he prays:

> To you, O God, be praise for this child, *N.*
> We hold him/her before you, begging mercy.
> Nurse him/her with your love
>   and keep him/her until the day of his/her baptism.
> Before you, O God, we are all infants.
> We praise you for life.
> We are dependent on your constant mercy.
> Nurse us, also, with the milk of your Word.
> Nurture us with the food of the Body of your Son.
> Keep us in your baptism
>   and so, by your grace,
>   receive us as your daughters and sons.
> Through Christ our Lord.

All: Amen.

A representative of the congregation brings up the book in which the names of baptismal candidates are enrolled, saying:

> That *N.* may be named with the only name by which
>   we are saved, enroll your child for baptism.

A parent writes the child's name in the book.

Then the presider lays hands on the child's head, saying:

> N., the Lord bless you and keep you
> until the day of your baptism.

All: Amen.

The final blessing and dismissal of the people follows.

STAGE THREE: PURIFICATION AND ILLUMINATION

Ritual Before Baptism

The purpose of prayer before baptism is to ask God's blessing on the coming event and to prepare the family for the baptism of the child and for assuming responsibility for the child's ongoing Christian initiation. Without such conscious commitment on the part of the family, baptism should not be celebrated. Prayer before baptism might well be integrated into the daily prayer of the family. Since several families may be preparing for the baptism of their children at the same time—for baptism is not a private family affair—each family should remember the other children and the other families at prayer. To this end the following Ritual Before Baptism is suggested.

Parent: Let us offer our prayers to God.

For . . . . , let us pray to the Lord.

All: Lord, have mercy.

All are invited to offer petitions. The following may be useful in certain circumstances:

> That our child may be kept safe until the day of his/her baptism, let us pray . . . .
>
> That our child may be born again in the waters of life and so be rescued from death . . . .
>
> That our child may drink from the water flowing from the side of Christ and never be thirsty again . . . .
>
> That our family be inspired to embrace our child with the faith of Christ and bring up the child in the life of the Church . . . .
>
> That, as a family, we may live the life of the baptized . . . .

> For the other families in our community who are preparing for baptism . . . .

Parent: Let us bless the Lord.

All: Thanks be to God.

Rite of Christian Baptism for Infants and Young Children

The purpose of the Rite of Christian Baptism for Infants and Young Children is to incorporate the child into the community of faith. The rite is the sacramental event by which the child, in receiving the Holy Spirit, becomes a child of God and a member of the Body of Christ. The emphasis in this rite is on the corporate nature of the Christian's identity as a member of the family of Christ. Because such an event is to be seen as an action involving the whole community, the baptism—except in extreme cases or medical emergency—should involve the children of a number of families and should take place in the Sunday assembly. Since the child will normally be welcome at the table of the Lord, it is good if baptism takes place immediately before the Liturgy of the Eucharist. Wherever possible parish baptismal festivals heighten the communal nature of the sacraments of initiation and call the children's families into communion with the wider Church. The Second Sunday of Advent, the Baptism of the Lord, the Easter Vigil, Easter Day, Pentecost, All Saints' Day, and the parish's patronal feast are all appropriate occasions for such baptismal festivals.

Immersion is encouraged as a more complete sign of our emergence into life from death and as an appropriate symbol of our trust that God will embrace the children in divine care. The postbaptismal rituals of the clothing, the anointing with chrism, and the enlightening are accompanied by words particularly appropriate to infants. As in ancient Church practice these baptized Christians are immediately confirmed with the anointing of the Spirit and are invited to share in the Eucharistic table.

> At the appointed time in the Sunday liturgy, preferably following the Liturgy of the Word, parents and godparents bring the children before the assembly. If the font is located as a communal focus, the entire rite takes place at the font; if not, a procession to the font follows the opening dialogue.

Presider: What do you ask of God's Church?

Families: Faith.

Presider: What does faith offer you?

Families: Eternal life.

Presider: For whom do you ask such faith?

The parents/godparents of each family answer in turn:

For N.

If there is no other Liturgy of the Word preceding baptism, a lesson is read:

Rom 8:9-11	The Spirit of God makes us new creations in Christ.
1 Cor 12:12-26	Baptism makes us members of one Body in Christ.
Gal 3:25–4:7	Through baptism we can call God "Abba."
1 Pet 2:1-10	Baptism anoints us to be priests and kings.
John 3:1-15	Nicodemus hears that we must be born again.
John 9:1-7	The blind man is washed by Christ and regains his sight.
John 15:1-11	We are incorporated together into the life of Christ as branches on a tree of life.

The presider may speak to the specific situation.

If there is to be a procession to the font, it takes place now and should be accompanied by an appropriate chant, e.g. Psalm 41.

The presider, with hands extended over the font, prays:

Lord, holy Father, almighty and eternal God,
with all your baptized people of every time and place
we praise you, we bless you, we sing your glory.

By your Spirit you created the universe,
by your Spirit Jesus was anointed King of our race,
and by your Spirit we mortal folk, formed of soil,
are called by your name and born into new life.

Over the flood waters, through the Red Sea, across
the River Jordan,
your people have been carried from death to life.

Pour now your Spirit upon this water.
Make it the birthing waters of a new and holy life.
Make it a lively spring to quench our aching thirst.
Make it a cleansing of what is soiled, within and
without.

Make it a flood sweeping us away from a deadly land
  into the dominion of your Son.
Make it a sign on these children of the name of
  salvation:
that Name in whom we are baptized,
the Name supporting the heavens and the earth,
the Name of the crucified and risen one,
Jesus Christ our Lord.
Amen.

The presider turns to the parents and godparents and asks:

Do you renounce Satan and all Satan's works and all
Satan's empty promises?

Families: We do.

Presider: Do you believe in God, the Father almighty,
the maker of heaven and earth?

Families: We do.

Presider: Do you believe in Jesus Christ, his only Son, our Lord,
who was born of the Virgin Mary, was crucified, died
and was buried, rose from the dead, and is now
seated at the right hand of the Father?

Families: We do.

Presider: Do you believe in the Holy Spirit, the holy catholic
Church, the communion of saints, the forgiveness of
sins, the resurrection of the body and life everlasting?

Families: We do.

Presider: Do you ask the life of faith for your children?

Families: We do.

The children are undressed for baptism.

The presider takes each child in turn and immerses or bathes the
child, saying:

N. is baptized
in the name of the Father and of the Son and of the
  Holy Spirit.

All: Amen.

Each child is then given to the godparents who dry the child with
a towel and then dress him/her in a white baptismal garment.

When the baptisms are complete and each child is dressed, the presider addresses them all, saying:

> Naked and helpless you came into the world.
> Wear these white garments and so be clothed in Christ,
> wrapped warm in the mercy of God.

The baptismal party then processes to the altar. Arrived at the altar, the presider stretches his hands over the newly-baptized and prays:

> O God, Father of our Lord Jesus Christ,
> we praise you for claiming your sons and daughters
> away from death and back to yourself,
> freeing us from the power of sin,
> and for birthing us to new life.
> Pour out your Holy Spirit upon these children:
> the spirit of wisdom and understanding,
> the spirit of right judgement and courage,
> the spirit of knowledge and reverence,
> the spirit of joy in your presence.

All: Amen.

The presider anoints the forehead of each child with chrism, saying:

> You were born a slave of sin.
> Receive this holy anointing and so become heir apparent to the promises of God.
> Be sealed with the gift of the Holy Spirit.

All: Amen.

The presider presents each family with a candle lighted from the paschal candle, saying:

> From the darkness of the womb you have passed into the darkness of this world.
> Receive this light of Christ.
> Be illumined by his resurrection
> to shine to the glory of God.

Since they are now baptized, the children are welcomed to the table of the Eucharist. The families turn to face the congregation and the presider says:

> These children, N. and N., have received the name of Christ
> and enjoy new life through the resurrection of our Lord.

> Receive them at the holy table as a member of the Body
>   of Christ,
> enlivened by the Holy Spirit,
> united with us in the family of God.

All: Welcome in the name of the Lord.

The presider may carry a child, or have the families carry their respective children, up and down the aisles and around the church, holding them high and showing the church its newest members. Meanwhile, the people may sing Ps 83, Ps 92, "Saint Patrick's Breastplate," or another appropriate chant or hymn.

The Liturgy of the Eucharist begins with the preparation of the gifts. The families of the newly-baptized might appropriately bring up the gifts.

STAGE FOUR: MYSTAGOGY

Baptismal Remembrance at Church

Christian baptism is the beginning and not the end of the Christian life, and everything flows from it. Whether as growing children or as adults, Christians need to set their roots in the waters of baptism. So it has been that throughout the history of the Church, the remembrance of baptism has been held up to the faithful, not only at baptism itself or at the Easter Vigil but at special baptismal anniversary celebrations. For all such occasions this Baptismal Remembrance at Church is suggested.

Presider: Let us rejoice together in our baptism into Christ,
            recalling our birth in the living waters
            and committing ourselves anew
            through the death and resurrection of Christ
            to God's covenant of life.

            Do you renounce Satan and all Satan's works and all
            Satan's empty promises?

All: We do.

Presider: Do you believe in God the Father Almighty?

All: I believe in God the Father. . . . (Apostolic Creed).

Presider: Do you believe in God the Son?

All: I believe in Jesus Christ. . . .

Presider: Do you believe in God the Holy Spirit?

All: I believe in the Holy Spirit. . . .

The presider blesses the people, saying,

Presider: May almighty God,
who has birthed us into new life,
quenched our thirst,
cleansed us inside and out,
carried us from a deathly land into the dominion of
righteousness,
and joined our death to the death and resurrection of
Christ,
sign you with the cross of Christ
and keep you safe, faithful until the end.

All: Amen.

Baptismal Remembrance at Home

Christians should know their baptismal date and mark the date with prayer and celebration. For children some festivity at a family meal is appropriate. The baptismal candle should be lighted. Any recalling of the baptismal images—white robe, illumination, anointing, signing with water—will help keep alive these symbols of faith. It is suggested that such baptismal remembrance culminate in the following prayer.

Parent: We drink from the Lord our God.

Family: We swim in the waters of life, we sail home to our God.

Glory be to the Father. . . .

Ps 100 is recited together, antiphonally, or responsorially.

We are God's people and we sing God's praises.

The lesson of Noah's ark is read. A children's Bible can be used, or Gen 6:11-21, 7:11-24, 8:6-20, and 9:8-17 read.

Parent: Let us offer our prayers to God.
For . . . let us pray to the Lord.

All: Lord, have mercy.

All are invited to offer petitions. The following may be useful in certain circumstances.

For *N.*, we give joyful thanks. That he/she may grow in grace and in knowledge of the love of God, let us pray . . . .

That our family may be kept safe in the ark of God,

That God our shepherd keep us in the pasture of mercy,

That God show love to all the people of the world,

That through the resurrection of Christ we may all live again,

The parent signs the child's forehead with a cross, saying,

The Lord bless you and keep you
and preserve you in your baptism.

Parent: This is the day the Lord has made for *N.*

Family: Let us rejoice and be glad in it.

It is hoped that these nine rituals surrounding the event of the Christian baptism for infants will, like the classic stages of precatechumenate, catechumenate, purification and illumination, and mystagogy, give an appropriate context to the sacramental entrance of infants into the Christian community.

5. REACTION FROM AN RCIA PERSPECTIVE

Robert D. Duggan

The provocative chapter by Andrew D. Thompson which anchors this volume has implications for adult initiation as well as for the future of infant baptism. In the reflections which follow, the author wishes to explore the suggestive comments of Dr. Thompson from the perspective of the Rite of Christian Initiation of Adults (RCIA).* Although his chapter concerned itself primarily with the context of the initiation of infants and young children, nearly all the materials presented from the human sciences also contain repercussions for the Church's initiatory *praxis* with adults.

Our experience with the RCIA is still too new for us to expect the kind of mature reflection that is possible with infant baptism. We have little more than a single decade of experience with the process of spiritual formation and liturgical ritual which the Second Vatican Council mandated for adults seeking entrance into the Church. Proposals for substantial adaptation would be premature at this point in time. What is more appropriate, it seems, is to begin a process of critical reflection on the emerging pastoral structures generated by the RCIA and to maintain a more tentative character in the remarks which follow. Our comments will follow the order of Dr. Thompson's chapter, dealing first with the issue he terms dialectic and then responding in turn to each of his seven principles governing the initiation process.

Dialectic and Human Development

Dialectic has been identified as integral to the process of matu-

* References are to the 1986 "white book" edition, published by the International Commission on English in the Liturgy, Washington, D.C.

ration and socialization and by implication initiation. One cannot help but be impressed by the scope of evidence amassed to reflect the consensus which exists in the sciences that "growth in the individual and in the community is strongly influenced by how they hold in tension the opposing forces of the dialectic." The initiation of adults, viewed as a form of religious socialization, must respect and build upon this foundational insight. Not to do so would be to build on the shifting sands of a disembodied spirituality rather than the bedrock of a strongly incarnational faith.

How then does the RCIA measure up to the challenge posed by this insight? Does it foster and facilitate growth-producing dialectic on various levels? Or does it collapse and repress the tensions which call a candidate and a community to adult conversion? Perhaps a better way to phrase the issue would be: how might the process of spiritual formation and the celebration of catechumenal rites be implemented so as to allow a dialectic of spiritual growth to occur at optimal levels? What do we need to do by way of pastoral care and how must we use the rituals of the RCIA, so that creative tensions are used to fuel growth and are neither blocked nor allowed to overwhelm? First, some general thoughts on pastoral care, and then some specific observations regarding liturgical ritual.

Aidan Kavanagh's now famous expression "conversion therapy,"[1] which he used to describe the nature of pastoral care during the time of the catechumenate, offers a valuable clue for an enlightened adult initiatory *praxis.* By evoking the therapeutic context, yet squarely targeting the Church's agenda as radical spiritual transformation, Kavanagh's image weds the human sciences with traditional *cura animarum* in an intriguing way. Pastoral care during the catechumenate, like good therapy, is not designed to shelter spiritual babes from the harsh realities of a hostile world. Rather, it is meant to equip one to encounter life's vicissitudes with maturity and confidence. This happens best when there is a gradual, progressive confrontation with whatever produces tension and conflict at the level of faith development. Dr. Thompson's chapter is filled with suggestive indications as to where one might explore such neuralgic points.

Two examples in the area of pastoral care typical of situations encountered in the catechumenal setting should help to concretize these remarks. The RCIA clearly indicates that the conversion journey of adult initiation involves an instructional component. Whether termed "a suitable knowledge of dogmas and precepts" (RCIA #75-1) or being "initiated into the mysteries of salvation" (#76), the intent of the Church is clear, namely, that systematic catechesis forms an important part of the community's ministry to the candidate. What is not made clear in the terse ecclesiastical prose of the Roman Ritual, however, is the *style* by which this is to occur. Is faith better served by a kind of indoctrination, whereby the candidate learns to accept revealed truth from a strongly authoritarian magisterium, or by a process which emphasizes more the community's questioning and common search under the guidance of the Spirit? And how ought pastoral ministers respond to the candidate who dissents, whose views place him or her in apparent conflict with official policy or teaching? If such conflictual situations are regarded as merely negative, as signs of a lack of faith or a rebellious spirit, then an atmosphere is created which invites regression not growth.

Style here reflects both feeling-levels and ideas. It can generate an atmosphere which allows, invites, and enables conflict where present to surface and contribute to growth. Or it can signal that questions are a threat, conflict an evil, and tension to be avoided at all costs—even if the cost be the loss of a more mature faith.

A second example can be given of sensitive pastoral care in the context of spiritual direction for RCIA candidates. A spiritual director may learn that a candidate has a family background involving strong racial prejudices, which are still part of his or her uncritically accepted values. Understanding how families influence attitudes and behaviors will be very helpful to the director, but so will a knowledge of how dialectic contributes to change. At some point the candidate will need to be confronted with the fact that his or her prejudices are antithetical to the Christian vision. How that confrontation occurs and how the candidate is helped to renegotiate personal values in light of the director's challenge, will be crucial issues of style. If healing is to occur, rather than just repression, the director will have to allow the candidate time and space to struggle with the issue and to embrace freely a new vision. Dr. Thompson's chapter reminds us that the tensions of the dialectic are to be played out gradually, lest they overwhelm, and that the challenge must be accommodated to the individual's level of readiness, lest the new stage of growth seem unattainable. Shrewd pastoral care of RCIA candidates will follow this wisdom.

In addition to providing a structure for pastoral care, the RCIA is also a sourcebook of liturgical rituals which mark the conversion journey underlying the process of initiation. Before leaving our discussion of the dialectic, it would be well to sample its implications on the level of ritual celebration. Dr. Thompson points out the importance of symbol in helping persons to grapple with conflictual situations. The RCIA contains several rituals which seem to highlight this dimension of the spiritual journey. Their importance needs to be recognized and appropriately celebrated. There are two occasions in particular provided by the Rite in which the candidate is asked to make explicit renunciation of whatever evils might attempt to ensnare him or her. At the beginning of the journey, during the Rite of Acceptance into the Order of Catechumens, an optional ritual of renunciation (#70-72) is provided, and at the journey's end immediately before baptism, all must renounce evil a final time (#217). Both these moments can be developed and used to highlight the spiritual realities experienced by the candidate under the form of conflict and struggle. The most developed statement of this reality, however, is to be found in the RCIA during the celebration of the Scrutinies. These contain the so-called major exorcisms (to distinguish them from the "minor exorcisms" described in #90-94) in which we find the Church's fullest ritual expression of the dialectic at the level of spiritual conflict. Let us explore these now a bit more closely with an eye to carefully highlighting the dialectical elements in the rite.

A thorough analysis of the language and structure of the Scrutinies is not possible in the limited scope of this article,[2] but such an analysis would reveal that the prayers and choreography of the ritual emphasize the mutual opposition between the forces of good and evil in a striking and forceful manner. The highly charged imagery of the prayers and the evocative body language of the Scrutinies focus on the tensions experienced by the candidate in the spiritual struggle. The language used describes ultimate stakes: life and death, light and darkness, faith and unbelief. It is as if the ritual concentrates in its most essential form the basic struggle of the entire Christian life.

We judge this positively in light of Dr. Thompson's chapter for the following reasons. We have seen that initiatory celebrations are a collaborative effort in which both the community and the individual are constructing shared values and identity. In the celebration of the Scrutinies (held during the community's Eucharist on three successive Sundays in Lent), great prominence is given to the basic developmental and initiatory issue Thompson terms dialectic, and it is done in a way that legitimates and positively contextualizes all of the life experiences which are symbolically subsumed in the celebration. Both the individual and the community affirm that evil's seductive lure, chaotic struggle with seemingly overwhelming forces, even the wounds and scars of failed attempts at good are part and parcel of the Christian life and to be expected in every spiritual journey. Finitude, fallibility, and human frailty are the raw materials out of which grace and conversion are fashioned. There is no room at Scrutiny time for a "will-power" Christian who masks refusal to grow with repressive behavior. In the work of the Scrutinies, to live is to struggle, to engage conflict is to risk, and to be thrown back at times of crisis on Jesus as Lord is to know salvation. The message is exhilarating as well as immensely reassuring. Needless to say the way these rites are celebrated must not belie the urgency and high drama of the issues with which they deal. Fidelity to dialectic as the "common thread" connecting Thompson's principles of initiation requires full, robust symbolic expression be given to the celebration of the Scrutinies.

Seven Principles Governing the Initiation Process

The intent of this section is to explore in more detail some of the implications for the RCIA of the seven principles outlined in Dr. Thompson's chapter. Once again space limitations will require us to restrict our remarks to suggestive comments rather than exhaustive treatments.

PRINCIPLE ONE: *Initiation is both an event and a gradual, developmental process by means of which the individual is socialized into the community.*

One important implication of this principle is contained in Dr. Thompson's discussion of the genetic epistemology assumed by the principle. The ongoing project of initiation involves less a "knowledge" that is a reified set of static truths and more "know-how" held in common, shared between generations, and constructed together. In all too many catechumenates today the operative model still seems to be under the control of religious educators whose bias is didactic, narrowly cognitive, and obsessed with content mastery. Under such a model there is little felt need for initiation to be experienced as ongoing process, once the "syllabus" has been learned. Yet "know-how"—that elusive, intuitive empathy for the Christian way—is something that is only gradually "caught" while other things are "taught." Furthermore, once the focus shifts from assimilating "knowledge" in the narrow sense to acquiring "know-how," the pastoral agenda shifts towards questions of meaning that are rooted in real life experience. Such questions are never finally resolved; they are the project of a lifetime, and the process of initiation is then seen as introducing one to a specifically Christian way of negotiating them on an ongoing basis. That is why already initiated members of the community are also engaged simultaneously in virtually the same task as the candidate: developing the "know-how" to live graciously and with Christian faith in a world of ever-changing life experiences. Seen in this way, it becomes crystal clear that a collaborative learning model is demanded for adequate catechesis during the time of the catechumenate. Any attempt by catechists to dump information—even if it *is* the "right answer"—into the heads of catechumens, is not just poor instructional technique, it betrays the very catechetical task it purports to accomplish.

PRINCIPLE TWO: *Initiation is a celebration by which the individual and community mutually construct their shared values and identity.*

This second principle is closely allied with the first, as should be evident from the remarks above. In his earlier discussion of dialectic, Dr. Thompson pointed out the built-in tension experienced in every initiatory process between the individual and the community, between separateness and togetherness, between excessive individualism that leads to isolation and exaggerated conformism that abdicates personal individuality. This tension can be the source of a tremendous creative energy for the community, whose RCIA process is able to harness rather than hamper its potential.

When new members are incorporated into a community, there should be an infusion of new life, new ideas, new aspirations. Initiation should transform not only the new members but the established community as well. Of course this will not be done without tension. Cherished ways of doing things will be questioned; sacrosanct customs will be inadvertently ignored; sensitivities will sometimes be offended. But in the give and take that transpires between those who love and trust one another, unforeseen possibilities can emerge as well.

This second principle speaks of a *mutual* effort to construct values and identity. Practically this seems to imply an RCIA process whose boundaries are quite fluid and whose style is highly interactive. Communication must flow; newcomers must hear and be heard; contact between persons must be frequent and intensive. There must also be opportunity for all involved to ritualize the new values and identity that are emerging out of this interaction. Anthropologists have alerted us to the importance of communal ritual in this regard, and the RCIA process needs to be rich in such celebratory moments. It seems important also to include both newcomers and representatives of the community in the development of those ritual experiences that celebrate their common values and identity.

Many a parish today is puzzling over what to do with the time of mystagogy. Here it seems is one promising avenue to explore. Responsibility might be given to the neophytes—together with some longstanding members of the community—to design a community-wide celebration during the period of mystagogy. The celebration could be primarily religious and held in church or social and held elsewhere. But the creative energies released by such a challenge and the networking with established parish resources that would inevitably be required would be powerful expressions of the newness in a community transformed by new members, as well as the familiarity still present in a community able to recognize itself in the faces of the neophytes. This suggestion might not be feasible in every situation, but it illustrates the potential of collaborative ritual-making.

PRINCIPLE THREE: *The emotional patterns of the initiate's nuclear and extended family are central, if not dominant, forces influencing the meaning of the ritual event and process of initiation.*

Dr. Thompson's cautions as to the centrality of the family and his presentation of that insight in the context of systems theory are very helpful reminders for those responsible for implementing the RCIA process at the local level. It seems fair to say that the primary focus of catechumenal ministry in parishes today is directed toward individuals *apart from* their family context.[3] With the exception of the occasional instance of an entire family seeking initiation together, most catechumenates treat candidates as if they were unconnected to any reality beyond the catechumenal group. This is a critical blunder, as Thompson has shown, since it is the family that is the "primary force" which "determines the emotional quality" of rites of initiation and their supporting process of formation (p. 77).

Much more attention than hitherto has been given needs to be devoted to engaging candidates at the level of family ties when ministering to their conversion journey. On the most practical level simply including family members more frequently as vital parts of the RCIA process would seem to be a basic starting point. Even more important, however, is making certain that the candidate explores thoroughly his or her "family story" in light of the religious changes taking place. By this we mean a look back at family patterns and history which have shaped—both positively and negatively—values, attitudes, and choices. What influences from parents or childhood contributed significantly to the candidate's spiritual journey? How can these be understood as times of grace? Where do they remain sinful and wounded, still in need of redemption? The candidate's "family story" should be told in terms of present relationships also and not confined to a glance backward at the family of origin. RCIA ministers need to help a candidate understand how the religious socialization process which he or she is undergoing will affect those closest to him or her. It is not an infrequent occurrence for a non-Catholic spouse who converts to Catholicism to feel frustration and disappointment at the Catholic spouse whose enthusiasm and interest in the Church appears less than the neophyte's. An exploration of these issues beforehand, within the context of catechumenal ministry, can help the candidate turn such experiences into challenges for further growth, rather than just sources of family tension.

The key in all of this is the ability of the catechumenal process to give to the candidate new levels of understanding and new tools with which to interpret and find meaning in life based on a Christian vision. Systems theory is simply the adoption of a new perspective. It is a new way of thinking about and seeing familiar realities. Its application to family, as to a multitude of other areas of life, has been fruitful because the new perspective opens the door to totally new approaches to problem-solving, creative imagination, and so forth. Dr. Thompson's suggestion that systems theory can enrich the ministry of initiation is well taken, but should not be restricted to family systems. In fact numerous other approaches might suggest themselves: a systems approach could be used to reflect on a parish's RCIA process or on broader parish structures. An individual's conversion journey could be analyzed as entrance into multiple new systems and strategies and consequences drawn out accordingly. What is common to all of these is the insight that *organization* is related to *interaction*, and once we step back to study how these variables work together, new possibilities are opened to us. For example understanding how the permeability of a system's boundaries influences the openness of the system can allow a community to look critically at its committees and discover why some are thriving with a constant influx of new members while others wither on the vine. Similarly parish ministers of hospitality or evangelization may suddenly realize how certain features of parish life unwittingly defeat their best efforts to attract newcomers. If, as Dr. Thompson asserts, the process of initiation is characterized by *complexity*, then the better our tools for understanding its many dimensions, the better able will we be to initiate effectively. Systems theory is one such valuable tool.

PRINCIPLE FOUR: *The individual's capacity for participating in the event and process of initiation depends on certain fundamental adaptive capabilities learned in the person's family of origin.*

The discussion in Dr. Thompson's chapter of how a person's family of origin shapes three qualities—configuration, coordination, and closure—which are crucial for an individual's ability to adapt and change might at first glance seem discouraging. The process of initiation hinges so decisively on a person's willingness and ability to change, that one might question how capable some persons are of full initiation when they come from families with low configuration, coordination, and closure. But the research reported must not be taken deterministically, since all of these abilities are quite relative. In fact the dynamic potential of the human person which underlies so much of current research into adaptive behavior is a strong argument on behalf of an optimistic approach to personal transformation.

What the research gives us, however, is a more realistic set of expectations and the ability to minister more sensitively to those with limited adaptive skills. The sciences remind RCIA ministers that some adults are simply less able to accept change with ease. This does not mean that they are incapable of conversion or initiation. It does mean that the process of religious socialization for them will likely be slower and more difficult. It also means greater demands on pastoral ministers from whom greater patience may be required, as they do remedial work with candidates who find change difficult. For such candidates a catechumenate extending for many months or years may be necessary, while for others less time will be required. It may also mean that parishes need to take more seriously the ongoing initiatory needs of those who have received formal acceptance into the community, but whose mystagogy must be prolonged, even for a lifetime.

Dr. Thompson suggests the importance of Christian story/myth which presents a holistic vision of one's relationship with the world as a possible bridge fostering adaptation in the initiatory process. We would underscore this point, adding the reminder that ritual celebration is the context in which Christian myth/story seems to convey its greatest formative impact. Once again we are reminded of how important it is to *celebrate* the conversion journey. The RCIA is not just a religious education program interrupted occasionally by some religious ceremonies. It is a powerful instrument of spiritual transformation, a sacrament in the most traditional Roman Catholic sense—effecting what it signifies. The symbolic enactment of an alternative world view which happens in Christian liturgy is not just "play acting" the reign of God. Rather, *it is an enactment* of the Kingdom proclaimed by Jesus, but realized here and now by the members of the community who *do* the ritual. The RCIA effects what it signifies, that is, conversion, for those caught up in the power of its ritual—those for whom "active participation in the liturgy" is not just the latest Church law but the tip of an iceberg that signals a massive commitment to the values and life-styles of Jesus' Kingdom.

The implication should be clear: yet another call for liturgical celebrations that are full and richly expressive, carefully planned, joyfully executed—as if our very being depended on their meaningfulness. Only those kinds of celebrations will carry enough impact to move forward into a new vision those whose family backgrounds have left them wounded, suspicious, isolated, and afraid. Only liturgies celebrated with deep conviction and inextricably linked to real life, gut issues will be able to turn around (con-vert) persons of low configuration/coordination/closure and allow them to enter a new (Christian) family that is "environment sensitive," a family whose values, visions, and skills are open, responsive, and fundamentally positive.

PRINCIPLE FIVE: *The level of trust which the participants bring to the event and process of ritualization is crucial for its outcome.*

This next principle helps us to explore more deeply how a person's makeup renders him or her more open or closed to the "conversion therapy" of the initiatory process. In particular by identifying three of the most important beliefs—trust in self, others, and the world—in an individual's belief system, research has targeted for us three areas that every catechumenal ministry will want to explore with a candidate. Spiritual formation would be shallow indeed if it were to ignore these crucial issues and concentrate instead on devotional piety or correct articulation of orthodox belief, however important these may be. Trust in self, others, and the world are the root concerns which Jesus preached in parable and action, and our proclamation of the Gospel must be no less attentive to those same issues.

However, Dr. Thompson's discussion of dynamic beliefs—that is, those which are functionally more important—might lead us in another direction as well. Functional importance—whether a belief is central, intermediate, or peripheral—has to do with whether or not change in a particular belief brings with it changes in the rest of a person's belief system. The three kinds of trust indicated above can safely be considered central beliefs for every person. But the concept might also be applied to other sets of religious beliefs. A case can be made in fact for the situation in which a relatively peripheral belief, for example, Latin as an unchanging official liturgical language, plays a functional role that is central. So the belief of many people in the old Latin Mass as the one and only way to worship on Sunday was changed by the course of events after the Second Vatican Council, and for them these events initiated a process of thinking which changed many other closely held beliefs. For these individuals a central belief had been changed, and the consequences were momentous. This example reminds us of how important it is that truly important issues form the core of a candidate's belief system. The catechetical ministry within the RCIA process then must concern itself with helping persons to move peripheral issues to the periphery and central issues to the center. Someone may be attracted to the Church by our position on the Roman primacy. But somewhere along the way catechesis must ensure that belief in Jesus as the Risen Christ finds a more central place in the candidate's belief system than does a particular style of papal ministry.

PRINCIPLE SIX: *The process of initiation presents an opportunity for the participants—parents, siblings, parish—to confront, adapt, and reconcile their disparate world views.*

The key to this principle is an understanding of crisis as a situation in flux which requires radical adjustment. Individuals, families, and even communities are according to this view "in crisis" during the process of initiation. We would not wish to exaggerate the extent of crisis/adjustment involved. Nor should one underestimate what is demanded for participants. As stated, this principle calls attention to the deep level of change required of participants in the initiatory process. Perhaps Dr. Thompson's greatest contribution here is the reminder that anything less than this deep level of change might be a way of selling initiation short. The RCIA calls us to an ideal vision of the Christian life, a vision whose demands we are constantly tempted to mute or deflect. Radical conversion is what the RCIA suggests must be at stake, for the community as well as the individual candidate. Inevitably this level of change will require reconciliation of disparate world views. All that has been said earlier regarding aptitude for change, openness to the new, and so forth, comes into play here. RCIA ministers must be sensitive to where their community or individual candidates are in terms of capacity for change. But no excuse should be allowed to silence the RCIA's prophetic voice regarding full conversion of heart and mind and soul to the Lord Jesus. Ultimately the commandment is one of perfect love, and we betray that saving work if we fail to utter it clearly and loudly, regardless of what will be demanded as a consequence.

PRINCIPLE SEVEN: *The effectiveness of the initiation process depends largely upon the levels of coherence which are to be found both within the child's nuclear family and in the primary religious community (for example, the parish). These levels of coherence can to some extent be empirically described.*

Two points important for the RCIA are being made in this principle. First, there are degrees of readiness (coherence) for supporting initiation that are possible within any given religious community. In other words some communities, by virtue of their organization and interactional patterns, their values and priorities, and so forth, will be better equipped and more responsive than others to meet the demands of implementing the RCIA. Second, it is possible to outline criteria by which that readiness can be empirically verified. This means a community could conceivably do a kind of "examination of conscience" as to its readiness/effectiveness in meeting the challenge of the RCIA.

Dr. Thompson describes two possible sets of criteria for such a task: how power/affection are shared and a crosscultural, anthropological framework for comparing value orientations. Both of these offer intriguing possibilities, but elaborating on their potential would be well beyond the scope of this chapter. More important is the task they remind us needs to be done. In fact pastoral care generally speaking has been remarkably devoid of the sort of objective evaluative criteria suggested here. At times it is as if the sacred nature of the ministry done in a pastoral context exempts it from critical scrutiny. If the cause is worthy and the motivation sincere, it can seem irreverent or lacking in faith to ask hard questions and criticize poor performance.

This principle provides a wholesome corrective to any attempt by pastoral ministers to cloak themselves in any sacral aura. Initiation is a task and a ministry too important to be left unreflected upon. As demanding and challenging as it may be for us to integrate the rigors of a scientific method into traditional approaches to pastoral care and liturgical celebration, not to do so would be a culpable failure of nerve or will. In fact Dr. Thompson's entire chapter and not just his last principle is a powerful plea and challenge to those involved in the ministry of Christian initiation to do just that.

The sketchiness of these remarks has been lamentable but necessary in view of the wealth of suggestive material in Dr. Thompson's chapter. If the reader is left with a sense of incompleteness, of a job begun but not yet completed, that is to the good. The reality in fact is exactly that: we have barely begun, but it has indeed been a beginning. What remains is the truly exciting task of shaping the future, not only of Christian worship but of the life of mission and ministry out of which all true worship arises.

Footnotes

1. Aidan Kavanagh, *The Shape of Baptism* (New York: Pueblo) 1978.

2. See my article, "Conversion in the 'Ordo initiationis christianae adultorum'" *Ephemerides Liturgicae* 97 (1983) 168–193.

3. For evidence of the importance of marital and family bonds in the process of conversion, see Dean Hoge, *Converts, Dropouts, Returnees. A Study of Religious Change among Catholics* (Washington: United States Catholic Conference, 1981) 43–71.

6. SPEAKING FROM EXPERIENCE:
WORSHIP AND THE SOCIAL SCIENCES

Stephen Happel

> About suffering they were never wrong,
> The Old Masters: how well they understood
> Its human position; how it takes place
> While someone else is eating or opening a window or just walking
>   dully along;
>
> —W. H. Auden, from *Musée des Beaux Arts*

Introduction: Social Sciences and Worship?

We use the word experience in many ways.[1] We let it name the unanalyzed data of our common life, the stuff of existence which passes through us seemingly without remainder. Used as a verb, to experience means to undergo an eventful moment, a time with serious personal content that has reversed our usual expectations. We speak from experience when we think we have something to say, rooted in events which have not only affected us, but which should affect our listeners. We advertise a job for a "person with experience," giving the word an evaluative edge, expecting applicants with expertise in the field. The expression an experienced man or woman can have connotations ranging from a high degree of professionalism to an extensive history of sexual performance. Appeals to experience in our lives, therefore, include everything from paying attention to data to deciding for or against a plan of action on the basis of existential witness.

The same spectrum of meanings affects the ways in which the social sciences are used in the theology of worship.[2] When we include anthropology, sociology, or psychology as part of an argument about the rites of initiation, we appeal to ordinary day-to-day experience, however analytically mediated. Several embedded logjams underlie current questions about the role of the social sciences in the study of worship.

To what kind of experience are we appealing? What role does the data of lived experience, whether of community or individual, play in determining the meaning of worship? Is it reductionist to include human experience in the study of worship? Is the language of belonging, socialization, psychological development, rites of passage, and personal discovery meant to replace the biblical language about dying, rising, and regeneration or the theologies of original sin, causality, character, and so on? Are we to determine what we ought to do in worship from analyses of what people have in fact done? Is the theology of initiation to be settled by arguments from family life?

The questions are intertwined. Since the problem affects not just worship but all of theology let us use the example of the evolution of Trinitarian doctrine from the Scriptures to Nicea.[3] The developed doctrine is not simply a report on consensus concerning a lengthy theological argument. Doctrines become normative for believers, resulting from and shaping specific practices in the sacraments, morality, and creedal formulae. Doctrines make a case for the nature of Christian experience and for what that experience ought to be.[4]

The descriptive and normative character of doctrinal statements often seems to conflict with the way in which social sciences are used in theology. The application of anthropology, for example, in studying the rites of initiation is not the use of a neutral, descriptive tool carving an inert religious identity. Rather, such social scientific presentations of Christian communities function both descriptively and normatively. By making the claim that the sacraments of baptism and confirmation are to be understood as rites of initiation, thinkers could be assumed to have reduced the sacraments to instances of another larger category. Since the initial applications of social science functioned as a hermeneutics of suspicion in relationship to religion, they tended to be reductionist, implicitly or explicitly overturning the doctrinal claims made within the framework of believers.[5]

A scientific parallel of Christian and non-Christian rites could collapse the former into the latter in the popular mind, raising still deeper theological questions. What is the relationship of divine grace to human cultures? Does God work "alongside" experience as another operator over and above human processes? Or does grace function within the normal range of ordinary processes, even if it transforms them along the way? Do the social sciences, therefore, provide prolegomena to theology, statements about human questions to which theology has the answer? Or are the social sciences operative within theology, providing an articulate framework for analysis of how the rites of initiation work, establishing a way in which they might be more effective? There are, of course, respectable theological adherents on all sides of this issue—whether confrontation, hegemony, or open-ended conversation.

In what follows, I need to assume that the relationship between the social sciences and theology has become an authentic conversation in which both contribute from their own specialties.[6] Not only does this assume that Christianity and the cultures of the world are not in a purely antagonistic relationship; it trusts that a mutually critical dialogue is desirable for both.

Productive conversations have a structure of their own:[7] they have an assurance that the other person is attentive; they focus upon the subject matter at hand; they consider the weight of the argument of each interlocutor; they entertain questions discovering the common pursuit; they attempt to bring out the strength of each speaker; and they recognize the possibility of change necessary to understand the world of the other. In this chapter social science and the theology of the rites of initiation will converse with (I hope) some equanimity.

I have two tasks. By arguing to include the social sciences in the study of worship, I will point out how these disciplines concretize the classical, abstract, and largely metaphysical theological understandings of instrumental causality. I will then point to some of the classic images and doctrines which are actually operative in the social scientific interpretations of worship used in this volume.

Instrumental Causality and the Social Sciences

St. Thomas Aquinas and the Sacraments

Scholastic language concerning sacramental effectiveness was developed in answer to conflicts in interpretation in the sources of theology. The long history of sacramental life, the symbols and narratives of the New Testament, the successive layers of Graeco-

Roman mystery religions (divinization),[8] Tertullian's legal formulae (*sacramentum*),[9] and Augustinian ecclesial vocabulary (character)[10] produced the need for consistency. Attempts to use a neoplatonic vocabulary of symbol (Pseudo-Dionysius, Hugh of St. Victor) proved helpful, particularly in their ability to relate the sacraments to cosmic hierarchies and to the spiritual developments of personal faith.[11]

St. Thomas Aquinas' use of Aristotelian vocabulary (agents, causes, effects, and instruments) to explain the operation of the sacraments seemed in its own day to be an intrusion of secular science into spiritual realities. Having articulated the way in which the supernatural strictly exceeds any human capacity to affect divine being, Aquinas was left with a tradition which maintained that the sacraments cause grace.[12] Human actions effect God's loving mercy; they are neither simple occasions of divine activity nor cognitive indications of God's presence. How could this be the case without supporting popular superstition or magic?

Aquinas' development of the notion of instrumental cause was an explanation of how the sacraments produced their effects. God is always the primary actor in divine human interactions. The principal cause always works through its own proper form.[13] Since grace is an inner effect, it could only be accomplished by God since only God can "be" there. Instrumental causes work through the power of the principal cause. An axe makes a bed through the design in the mind of the maker not of its own choice or energy. But the axe will also function by virtue of its own shape, weight, and sharpness. There are thus two sorts of effectiveness in an instrument, one through the intention of the primary actor, one through its physical characteristics.[14] Everything in creation is an instrumental cause of varying degrees and powers, cooperating in the achievements of governance or opposing the intentions of providence.[15]

The sacraments function as a particular kind of instrument for Aquinas. God works through the sacramental instruments to effect deeper connections with human beings. Yet they must work as well according to their own proper form. (It is the cutting edge of the axe which makes the bed.) Baptism uses water which washes the body by means of its usual properties; insofar as it is an instrument of divine activity, it transforms the soul.[16] Nor is this merely a parallel event. Because water as a created object is already an effect of divine action, its proper function (washing) discloses a divine effect (inner healing). Its created meaning becomes transparent to its redemptive power, something intended by God from the beginning but only available to us now in Christ.

This ability, however, of human objects to effect divine presence is due to the principal agent, Christ.[17] The humanity of Jesus is the primary created instrumental cause, originating the fundamental meanings of the sacraments in space and time. It is precisely the power of his passion, death, and resurrection operative in the sacraments which makes them able to grant healing and forgiveness. The stronger such a "conjoined instrument" is (for example, the hand as instrument of the body, Christ's humanity in union with the divinity), the more it can communicate this power to others, as Christ did to his disciples. As effective instruments of his own life, uniquely caused by divine love, the sacraments are both sign and cause. They perfectly express the divine intention to love the world as well as cause that presence to be available in the world. In this Christ's humanity works through its own powers.[18]

A certain ambiguity, however, appears in Aquinas' notion of instrumental cause. Since all realities below God are instruments, the notion explains too many things.[19] The idea of instrument must be determined in each instance. In Aquinas' understanding of the sacraments, the choice of an inanimate object as the example of an instrument has determined that human instruments, the ministers of the sacrament, will be considered in the same category as tools, water, bread and wine, or oil.

Aquinas recognized the difference by pointing to the way in which the ministers of the sacrament must have an intention to do what the Church does. Objects can be manipulated; human instruments move themselves.[20] Only by subjecting themselves to the principal agent are they able to be authentic instruments of Christ and the Church.

Moving themselves to be ministers of the Church requires only minimal attention. The intention of the whole Church is expressed through the use of the Church's words during the course of the sacramental celebration. However, to be able to speak the intention of the Church is not altogether within human power; it requires divine help.

The rite itself nonetheless cannot be vitiated by the one who unfaithfully administers it, since it is finally the work of Christ.[21] The "evil minister" can only empty the sacrament of the meaning over which he or she has control, just as the axe affects the quality of the outcome but not the presence of the bed itself. The divine intention embodied in Christ remains operative. A servant may give the master's alms for the wrong reasons, but the poor still receive the financial support.[22]

The conflict between precisely human causality in one's intentions and inanimate instrumentality should be clear. The latter is passive; the former requires human cooperation for effectiveness—at least not placing an explicit obstacle in God's way. But what of marriage where the explicit consent of the two ministers is required? Without their particular mode of human instrumentality, the sacrament itself is vitiated. Can the peculiarly human aspects of instrumentality not be brought forward to understand the way in which the sacraments work?

I have returned to Aquinas' attempts to explain instrumentality because they show us how a great thinker tried to incorporate the human character of instrumentality into his notion of sacramental efficacy but without much effect. The primary analogy remained the "thing" as instrument. Without forcing Aquinas into a contemporary mold, we can recognize that his use of instrumentality required at least three different sorts of explanation: one for Christ's role, one for the objects used during sacramental actions, and one for the human participants. Conflating or confusing the three kinds of instrument in favor of an inanimate common denominator only created difficulties.

Contemporary theology has studied the ways in which human instrumentality operates within sacramental life. From the thinness of things to the thickness of human meaning, sacraments function in an interpersonal way to cause what they signify. The polysemantic character of intersubjective causality and of the community as agent and common subject of the experience has required a shift in the explanations of sacramental efficacy. God is still the principal actor, but human attentiveness to things and people, the construction of metaphors, symbols and stories, the development of rituals as communicative devices, the tone, animation, and self-involvement of people, and the problems of deliberation, choice, and consequent action become the interrelated functions within interpersonal causation.

The shifts in our explanations for these experiences are not a crisis of faith but a crisis of culture.[23] The metaphors for transcendence are developed and transformed; the explanatory tools inside a scientific theology change. And though it is true that what we learn from and about God also shifts and changes, God remains the One who acts in love and justice.

A Contemporary Hermeneutic for Worship

Contemporary interpretations of worship use the explanatory concepts available to them for understanding the various dimensions of human meaning, whether affective, cognitive, constitutive, or communicative.[24] Simple bodily postures, manners, and public ceremony are the vehicles for disclosing the transcendent. If Aquinas used inert tools as a primary analogue, current theology understands the human instrument as a living community of individuals who interpret one another through multiple modes of self-expression.

Rituals are a particular genre of human communication. Midway between the routines which facilitate our daily lives and the obsessive neuroses which might cripple them, rituals enact formative gestures during crucial times in founded spaces.[25] Rituals identify themselves as Christian through their attachment to the history of Jesus of Nazareth. So for Aquinas the strictly supernatural effects of the sacraments are linked to their institution by Christ while on earth.[26] Initiation into mission (the baptism by John), healing, forgiveness, a community at table with sinners—each has its symbolic self-expression in Jesus' life. Each anticipates the eschatological trial of the Cross and the victory of the resurrection.

To study such symbolic genres as they are transmitted through liturgical texts (the *Didache*, Justin Martyr, Hippolytus, the *Ordines Romani*), we have the resources of literary criticism. What shape does a ritual text have? Who were the primary actors? What was the logic of the various speakers; who was the audience and what was the environment in which it arose?

Taking a cue from Paul Ricoeur,[27] we can discern many forms operative in Christian worship, such as hymnic wonder in which the fundamentally intersubjective character of the divine-human relation is enacted. From that prayerful admiration in the face of the Holy, we can see generated prophetic *praxis* in which the ecstatic "I" of the finite speaker becomes the "I" of God, proclaiming divine words to a people. Narrative exposition follows in which the awe of prayer and the *praxis* of personal symbolic witness attempt an answer to the question: why pray or speak in the name of God? Narratives tell themselves; tellers of tales efface themselves in the emplotment. From stories come demands for action, prescriptive laws, and the persuasive speech of the preacher and lawgiver. Then there are the thinkers or the teachers of wisdom, who insist on sorting out the ways in which Christian experience meshes with humanity's loves and hates and the cosmic suffering of the innocent. Finally, there are apocalyptic visionaries who experience only the lack of symmetry between worship and life, yearning for the embodiment of God's reign by the direct intervention of divine action.

The literary critical or formal questions begin the analysis since the ordinary symbolic world of story, plot, and character structures the human data that is negotiated through ritual. When the genre of ritual is operative, the participants are involved and engaged in the play of ritualized meditation, greeting or leave-taking, political diplomacy or religious conversation. The historical critical or factual questions operate later in moments of distancing in which the once and probably future participant is now a neutral observer, thinking about the data of the ritual itself. What happened empirically? What texts, if any, were used? How did the participants dress? Can the analyst locate the performance in its chronological and cultural contexts?

Anthropological and sociological explanations of ritual function after locating the data and its appropriate communicative category. The often highly articulated methods of each discipline provide explanatory categories for the ways in which rituals such as initiation share in the specific dynamics of change in familial and societal patterns. Formalized gestures and vestments, the "manners" of worship, appear in various cultures as styles of communication.

Just as Erving Goffman can analyze forms of talk in ritualized conversation, thus providing us with a contemporary context for sacramental dialogue,[28] so Victor Turner can study the rites of passage and pilgrimage in primitive or ancient societies to see their influence upon and reflection of Christian sacramental experiences.[29] Just as Aquinas' analysis of sacramental efficacy in terms of Aristotelian causes did not necessarily reduce the sacraments to human interaction, so social psychologists who might study the effects of the communications media on sacramental life are attempting to understand as precisely as possible the human factors which disclose God's action.

Psychological analyses provide us with some of the most helpful languages for understanding the self-involvement of the participants in their own symbolic behavior. The interpretations of faith development and its symbolic dimensions by Erikson, Fowler, and Kohlberg articulate the personal aspects of ritual. Why and how are people involved?[30] The affective dimensions of human interaction, especially those elements of conversion which become the vehicles for negotiating the community's awe and dread in the face of God, are studied. How do some rituals become the liminal experiences that Turner describes? Why do we assume responsibility for some stories and not for others? The therapeutic language of psychological catharsis can be especially helpful in this regard.[31]

Rituals, however, do not just embody the reigning ethos of a community, they also change it.[32] Worship, especially Christian worship, has a role in the establishment or rejection of the values for which it prays. During the course of worship, for example, in the Constantinian or Carolingian courts, particular political positions are both expressed and created. The symmetries and dissymmetries between the goals preached, proclaimed, and prayed in the sacraments and their actual embodiment require critical analyses. The social scientists with whom the theologians of worship must converse here are politicians and political theorists, economists and interpreters of what might be called involved aesthetics.[33] Worship is meant to be an emancipatory *praxis* through which a community not only confirms its already established Christian identity, but also challenges itself to enter further conversion.[34]

Worship is not politically, economically, or aesthetically naive; it argues, persuades, and embodies various schemes of social recurrence. Through its visions of the future, it redirects common desire, not in such a way that the community feels guilty for not living up to an ideal but by transforming the communion of believers, however incrementally, in the present. Through the sacraments we are enabled to love and established to complete a common work.

This social pragmatic level of interpretation recognizes the involved character of public discourse including religious rituals. It gets beyond the narcissistic attitudes of the theological or social commentator, the neutral observer, the ironic sport, or the fusive idolaters who substitute heroes or heroines for their true selves in the world. It also looks to the past; it asks about the production of a worshipping act. What was the demography and the modes of production of those who did or did not benefit from a particular act of worship? What images of the future did it present? Was the common desire anesthetized, mummified in nostalgic patterns of the past, or propagandized for ulterior political motives? Finally, through the use of an authentic critique from politics or economics, it becomes possible to propose within worship itself an enacted version of what the world would be like if . . . .[35]

All five interlocking levels of hermeneutical consideration must be operative to understand a text of worship. The literary critical, the historical critical, anthropological sociological, existential critical, and social pragmatic differentiations of interpretation provide us with a coherent series of questions to ask any liturgical performance or text. All of them tell us the truth about our worship; without one or another of them, we fail to understand our own celebrations. The answers to the questions assist the theologian in understanding the ways in which the human dimensions of the sacraments become the medium through which divine activity is present. The language of the social sciences does not explain the fact that God has chosen to act in Christ through these particular rituals; it attempts to understand how such action takes place within human horizons. In faith we know that what is mediated through the instruments is a Power not our own; how the Power appears is lived, known, and analyzed through finite energies of our own.

Conversion, Symbols and the Social Sciences

Finally, we shall look at some of the substantive themes which emerge when the community's symbols are interpreted through the social sciences. What relationship do these interpretations have to the classic scriptural formulations of sacramental experience? As our primary example we shall use initiation; as the primary themes we shall look at religious socialization and belonging, shifts in life patterns, and the questions of affective and social efficacy.

Socialization: Belonging to a Religious Culture

Contemporary religious education, sacramental catechesis, pastoral practice, and the structure of the Rite of Christian Initiation for Adults stress the way in which candidates for initiation are joining the religious family.[36] Entering new social patterns was the primary interest of the early Christian community. Less worried about adherence to sharply defined doctrines, the early community accepted only those who could prove their faithful adherence to an orthodox *praxis*. Indeed sponsors were assigned to assist them in that task. If classical theologies of the sacraments tended to ignore the ecclesial and historical mediation between Christ and contemporary practice in favor of the individual relationship and its mediations to Christ, current theologies focus upon the ancient patterns of ecclesial interaction.

The life, death, and resurrection of Christ were preached as a saving story, an event between a speaker and hearers, constituting a community as recorded in the Acts of the Apostles (3:12–4:4). The rhetorical form simultaneously created audience and preacher in a common discourse which issued in baptism as a commitment to that story.[37] The preached Word accepted through initiation constructed an assembly we call the Church. Theologies which interpret sacraments through social scientific paradigms understand that dynamic originating moment when the symbolic word and gesture establish mutual commitment, loyalty, and understanding.

The social matrix in which an individual Christian identity occurs is a pledge or promise of a divine communion, which God already shares within the divine reality. As beings in community, we struggle to enact the death and resurrection of Christ by bearing one another's burdens, sharing in an anticipatory fashion what we will one day become, the Body of Christ grown to full stature (Eph 4:11-16). It is not a coincidence that at the same time that Christians are recovering their essentially ecclesial nature, they are also beginning to retrieve the fundamentally communitarian character of the Christian God.[38] What God has always been, we will become. Divine life is already a mutuality in which knowing and being known, loving and being loved simultaneously form the perfect communion of individuals.[39]

The use of familial and societal processes to illumine the nature of initiation is not extrinsic nor a capitulation to middle-class culture. By discerning the adaptive characteristics of families and other intermediate infrastructures, theologians continue to understand the workings of human interdependence. Familial relationships establish that intermediary social microsystem which intervenes between individualist psychology and the macrosystems of politics, economics, and international diplomacy. Domestic interdependence as described and explained by the social sciences is in its turn confronted by the evangelical call for a discipleship of equals (Gal 3:28; 1 Cor 12:12-13), [40] a theology of collaboration over conflict (Matt 5:39), and the willingness to lay down one's life for one's friends (John 15:13).

Helping individual believers, therefore, to understand their cognitive and moral development in faith, socializing them into patterns of ecclesial awareness are thoroughly appropriate activities in the rituals of initiation. Encouraging and supporting families in their ability to develop children into full Christian adulthood promotes the middle level infrastructures of divine mediation between individual decision and societal transformation. Insofar as the com-

munity lives out that call, it participates in the divine nature itself
and discloses the holy community of love to the world. God's story
coincides more and more with human histories.

SHIFTS IN LIFE'S PATTERNS: CONVERSION AND SYMBOLS[41]

Our symbols and stories emerge from the deepest levels of our
interiority. Multivalent, they evoke, invite, and persuade us to participate in the multiple references to which they point. In contact-
ing our senses, symbols affect us intimately. Deprived of our
cherished secular symbols—a unique photograph of a beloved, for
example—we are diminished at the very center of our being.

Christian symbols, too, originate at the core of our interior lives.
Cleansed by water, rubbed with oil, caught up in darkness, blinded
by light, shaped by sound, and touched and pressured by impos-
ing hands, we are molded by the natural and historical meanings
such gestures and words have taken in our community. There is
always a reciprocal relationship between the inner conversion of
the believer and the symbol which is its expression. Sometimes it
is the symbol which evokes inner transformation; inwardness always expresses itself in a symbolic action, gesture, or word.

Christian conversion has many dimensions: moral, affective,
intellectual, and specifically religious.[42] The religious dimension
names processes of self-transcendence through which we fall in love
with God. Caught up in the love of a God we cannot see, we are
willing to forego all finite things or people to entertain the vision
of God. In that thirst for the Holy Mystery, the Uncomprehended
Other, there are cognitive, moral, and affective dimensions which
draw us on. Though intellectual, ethical, and emotional transformation can take place without religion, and religion does not ensure change in all other areas of our lives, a fully differentiated
transformation and integration of the self requires all.

In each case there is a need for an about-face, a shift in our sensibilities, our minds, our hearts, and our religious yearnings. Religious development is not a simple unfolding of an already established
solution, like an oak tree growing from an acorn. In moral conversion our choosing displaces itself from decisions made on the basis
of self to a basis in other-directedness; in intellectual conversion
our minds pay more attention to the subject matter than what it
can mean to us, knowing the conditions in our own thinking which
permit correct judgments. In affective conversion the loyalty of one's
sensibilities shifts from self to family, nation, and planet, even to

the point of generously giving oneself for a cause well beyond one's personal means.

Most conversions do not happen instantaneously (as Paul's seems to have, see Acts 9:1-22); they evolve gradually throughout our lives, unevenly operative in the differing dimensions of our histories. The social sciences provide us with developmental and collaborative paradigms for understanding the dissociation that can exist between intellectual convictions and emotional loyalties, moral impotence, and religious fervor. This dissociation can be understood as original sin, now not isolated to a legendary moment at the beginning of the human race, but as a continually perpetuated flaw in human beings who cannot sustain their own moral, intellectual, or religious development.[43]

What seems to teenagers like the end of their religious affiliation might be seen more appropriately as a crisis of affective loyalty. What was accepted literally or nominally throughout childhood and early adulthood may acquire the differentiation of emotion and affect, as one discovers one's loyalties, commitments, and centers of energy for action. The social sciences provide some of the vocabulary and grammar for understanding the conditions under which religious transformation might occur. No one ensures divine presence, but better that it should occur because of human cooperation rather than in spite of it.

Affective competence in a family or the levels of trust available in a given family system become important conditions for encouraging the appropriate interiorization of Christian symbols. The introduction of children or adults into a particular Christian ethos is a matter of educating them into ongoing orientations increasingly different from the secular world in which we live. As the nominal Christendom of the past two centuries disintegrates, it reveals the necessary voluntary acts on the part of those who wish to become Christian. The ongoing shift from selfishness to grace is not an abstract move; it requires a reevaluation of one's prior cultural bonds and a commitment to building new ones. Indeed it is rather like leaving one family for another, and rarely is the old family complacent about one's new allegiances.

Parental involvement in a child's baptism is therefore crucial to this expanding paradigm of Christian conversion. It was always a truism that it was the faith of the parents into which the child was being baptized; now that faith has gained a certain weight and involvement. The community asks for some parental responsibility in the ongoing conversion of the child, a willingness to recommit themselves to the sacraments of their own history so that they can become symbols for the child's life.

The Efficacy of the Sacraments: Social Conditions

In the classical theology of the sacraments, we maintained that unless there was a specific obstacle placed by the recipient, the sacraments were effective. They effected what they signified.[44] In some ways the development of the social and ecclesial mediations of sacramental action tells us some of the minimal and maximal conditions under which they can disclose God's presence. Minimally, of course, as long as there is some effort at mutuality, we can say that the Church's intention to embody itself in charity is fulfilled, but we can also see situations in which the human community might be so hatefully divided that the Eucharist could not be celebrated without scandal. The community would be divided against itself.

The negotiation of familial authority, the societal relationships of submission and dominance, the problems of interpersonal power and force, the ways in which affection contributes to overcoming the perplexities of separation and bonding can all assist us in better understanding the ways in which the sacramental life of the Church may express or overcome these patterns. For just as the sacraments are symbolizations of our current journey of conversion, they are also a share in the transforming power of God challenging the community to change. By assisting us in negotiating the social patterns of submission and dominance, they contribute gradually to an ecclesial body, sacramentally present to the world as illumination and prophetic prod.

Not only the negative minimal conditions, however, are at stake. Just as social scientific analyses of sacramental life in any given community can assist us in understanding the obstacles to full religious participation, so too they can provide access to the Christian imagination of how the world can be. They provide a sacramental prudence which knows what needs to be done to embody the good in specific situations. With sacraments as our guides, celebrations of our achievements, encouragement for further embodiment, and pledges of some final success, we find our common desires redirected toward the reign of God. Emphasis upon the social efficacy of the sacramental system returns the community to a recognition of how Christ's reconciliation of the world to the Father is incomplete until all one's brothers and sisters are included.

Footnotes

1. For the background of these comments, see Hans-Georg Gadamer, *Truth and Method*, trans. Garrett Barden and John Cumming (New York: Seabury/Continuum, 1975) 310–319.

2. See the controversy between Denys Turner and Kieran Flanagan in Denys Turner, "Sacrament and Ideology," *New Blackfriars* 64 (April 1983) 171–180, and Kieran Flanagan, "Turner on 'Operative Rituals': A Sociological Perspective," *New Blackfriars* 64 (September 1983) 425–441. For examples from quite differing perspectives, see David Power, *Unsearchable Riches: The Symbolic Nature of Liturgy* (New York: Pueblo, 1984) esp. 5–34, and William A. Van Roo, *Man the Symbolizer* (Rome: Gregorian University, 1981). For brief examples, see Roger Grainger, "The Sacraments as Passage Rites," *Worship* 58:3 (May 1984) 214–222; Elaine Ramshaw, "Sacramental Readiness and Psychology," *Liturgy* 1:3 (1981) 45–50; Franz-Jozef Noche, "Sakramente als Gesten: theologische Deutung von Zeichenhandlungen angesichts gegenwaertiger Erfahrungen," *Katechetische Blaetter* 108:6 (1983) 412–425. Contemporary surveys of the literature always point to this shift in interpretation; for example, see Augustin Schmied, "Perspektiven und Akzente heutiger Sakramenttheologie," *Wissenschaft und Weisheit* 44:1 (1981) 17–45; Kevin Irwin, "Recent Sacramental Theology: a Review Discussion," *The Thomist* 47 (1983) 592–608; and Henri Bourgeois, "Théologie Sacramentaire," *Recherches de Sciences Religieuses* 72:2 (1984) 291–318.

3. I am using the complex interpretation of Bernard Lonergan, *The Way to Nicea: The Dialectical Development of Trinitarian Theology*, trans. Conn O'Donovan (Philadelphia: Westminster Press, 1976) esp. 1–17, 105–137.

4. Bernard J. F. Lonergan, "The Origins of Christian Realism," *A Second Collection*, ed. William F. J. Ryan and Bernard J. Tyrell (London: Darton, Longman, & Todd, 1974) 239–261.

5. "So at bottom, it is the unity and the diversity of social life which make the simultaneous unity and the diversity of sacred beings and things. . . . It responds everywhere to one and the same need, and is everywhere derived from one and the same mental state. In all its forms, its object is to raise man above himself and to make him lead a life superior to that which he would lead, if he followed only his own individual whims: beliefs express this life in representations; rites organize it and regulate its working." Emile Durkheim, *The Elementary Forms of the Religious Life*, trans. Joseph Ward Swain (New York: Collier, 1961) esp. 460–461.

6. See R. Kevin Seasoltz, "Anthropology and Liturgical Theology: Searching for a Compatible Methodology," *Liturgy and Human Passage*, ed. David Power and Luis Maldonado (Edinburgh, Clark, 1979) 3–13; and the use of Goffmann in Aidan Kavanagh, *On Liturgical Theology* (New York: Pueblo, 1984) 136–150, though he argues that liturgical theology is far beyond socioanthropological studies, see p. 144.

7. See Gadamer, *Truth and Method*, esp. 330–331 and David Tracy's use of Gadamer in *The Analogical Imagination: Christian Theology and the Culture of Pluralism* (New York: Crossroad, 1981) esp. 101, 135–136, n. 8.

8. See for basic parallels, S. Angus, *The Mystery-Religions and Christianity: A Study in the Religious Background of Early Christianity* (London: Murray, 1928)

and Hugo Rahner, *Greek Myths and Christian Mystery*, trans. Brian Battershaw (New York: Harper & Row, 1963).

9. Dmitri Michaelidès, *Sacramentum chez Tertullien* (Paris: Etudes Augustiniennes, 1970).

10. Nicholas M. Haring, "St. Augustine's Use of the Word 'Character,'" *Medieval Studies* 14 (1952) 79–97 and his "The Augustinian Axiom 'Nulli Sacramento Injuria Facienda Est,'" *Medieval Studies*, 16 (1954) 87–117.

11. Marie-Dominique Chenu, "The Symbolist Mentality," in *Man, Nature and Society in the Twelfth Century*, trans. Jerome Taylor and Lester K. Little (Chicago: University of Chicago Press, 1968) 99–145.

12. "Sacramenta novae legis per aliquem modum gratiam causare." S.T. III, 62, 1 corp.; "quaedam virtus instrumentalis ad inducendum sacramentalem effectum. Et haec quidem virtus proportionatur instrumento." S.T. III, 62, 4 corp.; "gratia sacramentalis addit super gratiam communiter dictam, et super virtutes et dona, quoddam divinum auxilium ad consequendum sacramenti finem." S.T. III, 62, 2 corp.

13. "Principalis . . . operatur per virtutem suae formae, cui assimilatur effectus." S.T. III, 62, 1 corp. Note that the effect is assimilated to the principal cause.

14. S.T. III, 62, 1 corp., where the effect is attributed to the primary cause; yet in ad 2um, this is refined: "instrumentum habet duas actiones . . ."

15. See Bernard Lonergan, *Grace and Freedom: Operative Grace in the Thought of St. Thomas Aquinas*, ed. J. Patout Burns (London: Darton, Longman & Todd, 1971) 80–84.

16. "Sed ad sanctificationem non ordinantur ex aliqua virtute naturaliter indita, sed solum ex institutione divina" S.T. III, 60, 5, ad 2; "lectus non assimilatur securi, sed arti quae est in mente artificis." S.T. III, 62, 1 corp., ad 1; "similiter sacramenta corporalia per propriam operationem quam exercent circa corpus, quod tangunt, efficiunt operationem instrumentalem ex virtute divina circa animam." III, 62, 1, ad 2.

17. S.T. III, 64, 3 corp.

18. S.T. III, 62, 5 corp.; 64, 3 corp.

19. Lonergan, *Grace and Freedom* 82.

20. "quodammodo movet seipsum, in quantum sua voluntate movet membra ad operandum." S.T. III, 64, 8, ad 1.

21. "Christus operatur in sacramentis et per malos . . . et per bonos . . ." S.T. III, 64, 5, ad 2.

22. S.T. III, 64, 10, ad 3.

23. See my article "Classicist Culture and the Nature of Worship," *The Heythrop Journal* 21 (July 1980) 288–302.

24. The vocabulary that follows has its origins in a reflection on Ron L. Grimes, *Beginnings in Ritual Studies* (Lanham, Md.: University Press of America, 1982) esp. 35–51 and Bernard Lonergan, *Method in Theology* (London: Darton, Longman & Todd, 1972) 76–85; a more extensive interpretation of this material may be found in my article "Symbols that Redirect our Desires," in *Desires of the Human Spirit*, ed. Vernon Gregson (New York: Paulist, forthcoming).

25. Grimes, *Ritual Studies*, 55.

26. "solum ex institutione divina," S.T. III, 60, 5, ad 2, where "institutio divina" means through Christ, S.T. III, 64, 3 corp.

27. Paul Ricoeur, "Toward a Hermeneutic of the Idea of Revelation," *Harvard Theological Review* 70 (1977) 1–37.

28. Erving Goffman, *Forms of Talk* (Philadelphia: University of Pennsylvania Press, 1981) esp. 5–159.

29. Victor Turner, *The Ritual Process: Structure and Anti-Structure* (Chicago: Aldine, 1969) and Victor Turner and Edith Turner, *Image and Pilgrimage in Christian Culture: Anthropological Perspectives* (Oxford: Blackwell, 1978) and the application of Turner in Margaret Mary Kelleher, "Liturgy: An Ecclesial Act of Meaning," *Worship* 59:6 (November 1985) esp. 488–491.

30. See the interpretation of developmental psychology in relationship to faith and morality in Stephen Happel and James J. Walter, *Conversion and Discipleship: A Christian Foundation for Ethics and Doctrine* (Philadelphia: Fortress, 1986) 53–82.

31. See T. J. Scheff's *Catharsis in Healing, Ritual, and Drama* (Berkeley: University of California Press, 1979) esp. 1–179.

32. Stephen Happel, "Whether Sacraments Liberate Communities: Some Reflections upon Image as an Agent in Achieving Freedom," *Lonergan Workshop V,* ed. Fred Lawrence and Charles C. Hefling, Jr. (Chico, Calif.: Scholars Press, 1985) 197–217.

33. Here we need to point to Marxist writers on aesthetics such as Louis Althusser (*For Marx*, trans. Ben Brewster [London: Allen Lane, 1969]), Terry Eagleton, (*The Function of Criticism: From the Spectator to Poststructuralism* [London: Verso, 1984]; *Literary Theory: an Introduction* [Minneapolis: University of Minnesota Press, 1983]), Fredric Jameson, (*The Political Unconscious: Narrative as a Socially Symbolic Act* [Ithaca: Cornell University Press, 1981]), Frank Lentricchia, (*Criticism and Social Change* [Chicago: University of Chicago Press, 1983]), and Edward Said (*The World, the Text and the Critic* [Cambridge, Mass.: Harvard University Press, 1983]).

34. See the transformational motif assumed by Susan A. Ross, "The Aesthetic and the Sacramental," *Worship* 59:1 (January 1985) 2–17, basing itself on Juan Luis Segundo, *The Sacraments Today*, trans. John Drury (New York: Orbis, 1974). Note the contrast with Cynthia Bourgeault, "The Aesthetic Dimension in the Liturgy: a Theological Perspective for Literary Historians," *The University of Toronto Quarterly* 52:1(1982) 9–19.

35. Upon completion of this paradigm, I have found a similar system for organizing interpretive procedures in William M. Thompson, *The Jesus Debate: A Survey and Synthesis* (New York: Paulist, 1985) 79–89, though the level of transformative *praxis* appears at another point in the text, see 401–427.

36. See, for example, Virginia Burke, "The Role of the Family in Preparing Children for the Sacraments," *Our Sunday Visitor 69* (April 19, 1981) 14; Greg Dues, "Hints for Parents in Sacamental Preparation Programs," *The Catechist* 18 (January 1985) 16–18; Roland Hirschauer, "Liturgie in der Familie," *Katechetische Blaetter* 109:10 (1984) 728–732.

37. On the characteristics of rhetoric, see Chaim Perelman, *The Realm of Rhetoric*, trans. William Kluback (Notre Dame: University of Notre Dame Press, 1982).

38. For a popular survey, see Joseph Bracken, *What Are They Saying about the Trinity?* (New York: Paulist, 1979) and for a constructive presentation and excellent critique of contemporary positions, see William Hill, *The Three-Personed*

God: The Trinity as a Mystery of Salvation (Washington: Catholic University of America Press, 1982).

39. See Bernard Lonergan, "The Mediation of Christ in Prayer," *Method: Journal of Lonergan Studies* 2 (March 1984) 1, 1–21 and James Robertson Price, "Triune Mysticism and Politics," *Lonergan Workshop VI*, ed. Fred Lawrence and Charles C. Hefling, Jr. (forthcoming).

40. Elisabeth Schüssler Fiorenza, "The Biblical Roots for the Discipleship of Equals," *Journal of Pastoral Counselling* 14 (Spring, Summer 1979) 7–15.

41. For a lengthier treatment of this topic, see Stephen Happel and James J. Walter, *Conversion and Discipleship* esp. 7–25, and Walter Conn, *Conversion* (Ramsey, N.J.: Paulist, 1986).

42. Bernard Lonergan, *Method in Theology* esp. 237–247.

43. Bernard Lonergan, *Insight: A Study of Human Understanding* (New York: Longmans, 1967) 666–668.

44. See the contemporary compendia of Bernard Leeming, *Principles of Sacramental Theology* (Westminster, Md.: Newman Press, 1963, 2nd ed.) 6–7, 122–125 and William A. Van Roo, *De Sacramentis in Genere* (Rome: Gregorian University Press 1960) 237–238, 343–345.

Index